I0476124

Return to table of contents

Chapter 1: Doing Business In Mauritius

- Market Overview
- Market Challenges
- Market Opportunities
- Market Entry Strategy

Market Overview   Return to top

Mauritius, a small island nation of 1.2 million people 500 miles east of Madagascar, is one of the most competitive, stable, and successful economies in Africa. With a 2013 Gross Domestic Product (GDP) of USD 11.9 billion and per capita GDP of over USD 9,000, Mauritius is ranked as an upper-middle income country by the World Bank. Mauritius' small land area of only 2,040 square kilometers understates its importance to the Indian Ocean region as it controls an Exclusive Economic Zone of more than 2 million square kilometers, one of the largest in the world.

For the sixth consecutive year, the World Bank's 2014 Doing Business report ranks Mauritius first among African economies (20th worldwide) in terms of overall ease of doing business. The 2014 Index of Economic Freedom, published annually by the

Heritage Foundation, ranks Mauritius as the 8th freest economy in the world and 1st out of the 48 countries of Sub-Saharan Africa. Mauritius also topped the list of Africa's best-governed nations for the seventh consecutive year according to the 2013 Mo Ibrahim Index of African Governance

Mauritius is a parliamentary democracy based on the British Westminster system. This system has engendered democratic values and provided for considerable political stability throughout Mauritius, contributing to its steady economic growth since independence in 1968.

The most important sectors of the Mauritian economy are:

- Tourism
- Textiles
- Sugar
- Financial Services

In recent years, the following sectors have emerged, attracting substantial investment from both local and foreign investors:

- Information and Communications Technology (ICT)
- Seafood
- Hospitality and property development
- Healthcare
- Education and training

In 2006, the Government of Mauritius embarked on a bold economic reform program aimed at opening the economy, facilitating business, improving the investment climate, and mobilizing foreign direct investment and expertise. The reforms helped the economy to resist the initial shocks of the global recession and Eurozone crisis and set the stage for Mauritius to resume accelerated growth in 2010. However, the deepening of the Eurozone crisis in subsequent years affected key sectors such as the tourism, textile, and the offshore financial sectors, which depend heavily on the European markets, and resulted in a steady deceleration of real GDP growth from 4.2 percent in 2010 to 3.2 percent in 2013. However, in view of the improving external environment, the IMF estimates real GDP growth will improve to 3.7 percent in 2014.

Also in 2006, Mauritius and the United States signed a Trade and Investment Framework Agreement (TIFA), aimed at strengthening and expanding trade and investment ties between the two countries.

The United States is Mauritius' third largest export market but only 15th as a source of imports. Principal imports from the United States include:

- Plastics (silicone liquid/gel)
- Agricultural/construction/industrial machinery and equipment
- Medical and surgical instruments
- Precious stones and jewelry
- Aircraft parts
- Automatic data processing machines

- Industrial chemicals

Mauritian exports to the United States include:

- Apparel
- Sugar
- Non-industrial diamonds and jewelry articles
- Primates
- Sunglasses
- Tuna loins
- Processed Specialty Foods

Mauritian exports are eligible for preferential access to markets of the South African Development Community (SADC), the Common Market for Eastern and Southern Africa (COMESA), the Indian Ocean Commission (IOC), Europe (under the EU-East Africa Economic Partnership Agreement), and the United States (under the African Growth and Opportunity Act-AGOA). Mauritius also has free trade agreements with Pakistan and Turkey. It is also in the process of finalizing a Comprehensive Economic Cooperation and Partnership Agreement with India.

Market Challenges   Return to top

There are no specific barriers for U.S. firms entering the Mauritian market. The small size of the Mauritian market (1.2 million people) and the vast distance (10,000 miles) between Mauritius and the United States negatively influence freight costs and therefore the competitiveness of U.S. products vs. their European and Asian counterparts. U.S. firms entering the Mauritian market must contend with well-established European and Asian competitors. Consumers are generally price sensitive, although middle to high-income consumers are willing to pay a higher price for quality.

The stated government policy is to act as a facilitator to business, leaving production to the private sector. However, the government controls key utility services, including electricity, water, waste water, postal services, and television broadcasting. The State Trading Corporation controls imports of rice (non-basmati), wheat flour, and petroleum products, while the Agricultural Marketing Board controls imports of potatoes, onions, corn, and some spices that compete with locally grown produce. An administered price regime remains in place for a few basic goods (e.g. wheat flour, bread, cooking gas, canned fish, pharmaceuticals, etc.), the prices to which the low-income section of the population is most sensitive.

Market Opportunities   Return to top

Factors benefiting U.S. exporters/investors include:

- A history of political and social stability and sound economic management
- A strong and dynamic private sector
- A sophisticated banking and financial services sector.
- A well-developed legal and commercial framework

- Double Taxation Avoidance Treaties and Investment Promotion and Protection Agreements signed with numerous African countries that make Mauritius an excellent platform for investment into Africa.
- GOM's infrastructure investment program of USD 4 billion over the next decade.

In general, the best prospects for exports are in capital goods and services. Of particular note are:

- Renewable and clean energy
- Medical equipment and healthcare services
- Plastics (silicone liquid/gel)
- Drugs/pharmaceuticals
- Energy efficient building design and equipment
- Port and container handling equipment
- Hotel and restaurant equipment
- Safety/security equipment
- Agricultural/construction/industrial and machinery
- Air conditioning/refrigeration equipment
- Traffic lights, speed cameras, and electronic toll systems
- Telecommunications and Information Technology
- Textile machinery and equipment
- Light Railway Transit system
- Franchising
- Consultancy services for seaport and airport infrastructure, energy, and ocean economy projects

Agricultural and food sector opportunities include:

- Wheat
- Crude vegetable oil
- Corn and soybean for animal feed
- Seeds (potato, onion and other vegetable seeds; fruit and flower seeds)

Market Entry Strategy Return to top

To enter the Mauritian market, the use of a locally established agent or distributor is strongly recommended. Mauritians are bilingual in English and French. Mauritian Creole, a modified form of French, is the mother tongue of most Mauritians.

Distribution of goods is uncomplicated given Mauritius' size: 42 miles north to south, and 28 miles east to west. Goods are distributed through the standard channels of importers, wholesalers, retailers, and supermarkets.

We recommend that U.S. firms join a local partner while bidding for large government projects in Mauritius. In evaluating bids, the authorities often give points to bidders that have a local partner they can contact, especially in projects requiring after-sale support services.

The Embassy's Economic/Commercial Section offers a variety of services designed to assist U.S. firms develop their market entry strategy and facilitate their export experience in Mauritius. For detailed information on these services, we recommend you visit the Embassy website at http://mauritius.usembassy.gov and click on the Business tab. The Economic/Commercial Section in Port Louis partners with the U.S. Commercial Service in Johannesburg, South Africa, to expand the commercial resources we have available to interested parties. For a more comprehensive list of commercial services available to U.S. businesses, we recommend you visit their website at http://www.buyusa.gov/southafrica/en and click on "Services to U.S. Businesses."

Web Resources

http://mauritius.usembassy.gov

http://www.buyusa.gov/southafrica/en

Return to table of contents

Return to table of contents

Chapter 2: Political and Economic Environment

For background information on the political and economic environment of Mauritius, please click on the link below to the U.S. Department of State Background Notes.

http://www.state.gov/r/pa/ei/bgn/2833.htm

Return to table of contents

Return to table of contents

Chapter 3: Selling U.S. Products and Services

- Using an Agent or Distributor
- Establishing an Office
- Franchising
- Direct Marketing
- Joint Ventures/Licensing
- Selling to the Government
- Distribution and Sales Channels
- Selling Factors/Techniques
- Electronic Commerce
- Trade Promotion and Advertising
- Pricing
- Sales Service/Customer Support
- Protecting Your Intellectual Property
- Due Diligence
- Local Professional Services
- Web Resources

Using an Agent or Distributor   Return to top

The use of an established agent or distributor is strongly recommended.
More than 200 U.S. companies/products are represented by local agents and distributors. For products requiring servicing, qualified personnel and a reasonable supply of parts are essential. The Embassy can assist U.S. firms in identifying an agent or distributor though our International Partner Search or Gold Key Service. Interested parties must apply through the U.S. Commercial Service at the American Consulate in Johannesburg, South Africa. For additional information, please visit our Embassy website at http://mauritius.usembassy.gov or the U.S. Commercial Service Southern Africa site http://www.buyusa.gov/southafrica/en/servicestouscompanies.html.

Establishing an Office Return to top

The World Bank's 2014 Ease of Doing Business report ranks Mauritius first in Africa for the sixth year in a row in terms of overall ease of doing business. The Business Facilitation Act of 2006 simplified the business licensing process with respect to starting a business and allowed businesses to start operations within three days of incorporation. Before starting operations, businesses must register with the Registrar of Companies. Regulations governing incorporation are contained in the Companies Act of 2001, which provides for the setting up of various types of companies. A list of the types of companies, as well as details regarding their incorporation in Mauritius, can be obtained at http://companies.gov.mu/.

The most common type used by foreigners is the private limited company. After receipt of a certificate of incorporation from the Registrar of Companies, all companies must register their business activities with the Board of Investment (BOI, http://www.investmauritius.com), the government's business facilitation and investment promotion agency, in order to apply for an occupation permit (work and residence permits combined) and other services offered to investors.

Any person, either alone or together with another person, may apply for the incorporation of a company. A proposed company may choose to have a constitution, which need not be embodied in a notarial deed. The Companies and Businesses Registration Integrated System provides for the electronic submission of applications for the incorporation of companies and of the National Business Registration Number. The on-line application form for the incorporation of a company is available at http://mns.mu/cbris-companies.php.

Franchising Return to top

Franchising in Mauritius is predominantly, but not exclusively, found in the fast food sector. With per capita income of over USD 9,000 and two-income families leading increasingly hectic lives, the market for family restaurants and similar conveniences is growing. Kentucky Fried Chicken, Pizza Hut, and McDonalds have been operating in Mauritius for several years. A number of South African franchises such as Nando's, Steers, Debonair Pizza, Spur, and Ocean Basket are also present in Mauritius. Coca-Cola and Pepsi products are produced under license by Mauritius Breweries Ltd and Quality Beverages, respectively. Many of the resorts and hotels present in Mauritius, such as Holiday Inn, are also operated under franchise agreements.

Direct Marketing Return to top

Direct marketing is limited to big-ticket items requested through government tenders. A few cosmetic, health, as well as house cleaning products are sold directly to consumers through visits to households or offices. Overseas shopping by mail order and internet is not common due to the small size of the island and the high cost of shipping goods internationally.

Joint Ventures/Licensing Return to top

Joint ventures are used mostly for construction and engineering projects. Foreign architects are required to enter into a joint venture with a Mauritian architect or firm to work on local projects. Licensing agreements, including royalties, are typically negotiated between the local firm and the foreign partner. Local companies are currently manufacturing a number of products, ranging from beverages to toiletries, under licenses.

Selling to the Government Return to top

Major government contracts are handled through an autonomous Central Procurement Board. Government procurement regulations are available at http://www.gov.mu/portal/goc/pposite/file/pporeg.pdf. The Procurement Policy Office is responsible for formulating policies and issuing directives for the operation of a transparent and efficient public procurement system.

Tender notices are published in the Government Gazette and local media. They can also be accessed from the following Government of Mauritius web site: http://publicprocurement.gov.mu/Pages/default.aspx. Tenders open to foreign participation are transmitted by the Embassy to the U.S. Department of Commerce, which in turn disseminates them to the U.S. business community through U.S. Export Assistance Centers and other relevant agencies. Successful foreign bidders generally work with local partners in pursuing major contracts.

Distribution and Sales Channels Return to top

Distribution of goods is relatively uncomplicated once goods arrive on the island given Mauritius' size: 42 miles north to south, and 28 miles east to west. Port Louis has a population of 155,000 and is the island's commercial center. There are four other major towns. Goods are distributed through the standard channels of importers, wholesalers, retailers, and supermarkets.

Selling Factors/Techniques Return to top

Effective advertising, competitive pricing, prompt delivery and reliable after-sales servicing are critical. Companies wishing to introduce new products into the Mauritian market require market research to identify potential customers, buying patterns, and preferences.

In general, food products, especially prepared/processed food, must be adapted to local tastes and conditions. To cater to the Muslim community (17 percent of the population), provision must be made for "halal" processing (slaughtered according to Muslim rites). Many Hindu Mauritians (52 percent of the population) do not eat beef.

Electronic Commerce Return to top

E-commerce on the island is quite limited. The speed and bandwidth required for modern e-commerce transactions are lacking in some areas. Mauritians still use websites more for information gathering than for purchasing. Although the tariffs for ADSL and wireless internet connections have gone down significantly recently, internet services are still not affordable to all. Payment by credit cards, though, is very popular and is rapidly replacing cash payment, particularly in malls and supermarkets. Internet banking is relatively new but is increasingly being used by consumers.

Trade Promotion and Advertising   Return to top

The advertising industry in Mauritius is quite sophisticated and advertising is essential to the successful launch of a product or service in Mauritius. U.S. exporters should be prepared to provide promotional support to their agents/distributors, particularly when introducing a product to the market. Advertising can be in English, French, or Creole (the local dialect) but French and Creole are more popular.

Major media outlets include television, radio, newspapers, magazines, and billboards. The deregulation of the airwaves has introduced more competition via three independent radio stations. Television broadcasting, however, has not been liberalized and the Mauritius Broadcasting Corporation is the government-run national television company. Television advertising is the most effective way to reach consumers. Consumer goods account for most advertising, followed by durables and services (banking, insurance, information technology, education).

There are about 200 advertising agencies in Mauritius. The Association of Advertising Agencies of Mauritius comprises the 15 largest agencies and accounts for 70 percent of the market. They provide a full range of services from concept to the final product, including media planning, market surveys, and creation of advertising materials. Advertising agencies normally derive a 20 percent commission from any media booking. Multinational companies tend to work on a service fee basis rather than commission. The 15 largest agencies may be contacted through the association at:

Association of Advertising Agencies of Mauritius
P.O. Box 522
Port Louis, Mauritius
Tel: +230 286-7330; Fax: +230 286-7334
Email: aaamauritius@intnet.mu
Web: http://www.aaamauritius.mu

There are four major daily newspapers and many weeklies. Most are in French but they do carry some articles and advertisements in English. L'Express Weekly and new business magazines include:

- L'Express (daily) http://www.lexpress.mu
- Le Mauricien (daily) http://www.lemauricien.com
- Le Defi Quotidien (daily) http://www.ledefimedia.info
- Le Matinal (daily) http://www.lematinal.com
- Week-end (weekly) http://www.week-end.mu
- Business Magazine (weekly) Email: busmag@orange.mu

Pricing Return to top

The Mauritian market is generally price sensitive, although middle and high-income brackets increasingly look for quality.

Prices are generally market-determined. However, the government controls prices and/or markups on a limited number of goods as a form of social protection to vulnerable groups. The product categories currently subject to the maximum price regime are:
- Petroleum products
- Cooking gas (for domestic use only)
- Wheat flour
- Rice (other than basmati)
- Bread

Maximum markups ranging from 17 - 45 percent apply to pharmaceuticals, timber, tires, infant milk, canned fish (pilchards), corned beef/mutton, and imported fresh fruits.

Mauritius applies a 15 percent Value Added Tax (VAT) on all goods and services, except for some basic staple food items, medical and dental services, most pharmaceuticals, and educational and training services.

Sales Service/Customer Support Return to top

After-sales servicing and availability of spare parts are essential for successfully marketing certain goods, particularly machinery and equipment. Most importers/distributors of domestic appliances and electronic goods have a workshop for servicing and sale of spares. U.S. manufacturers should be prepared to train local staff to provide efficient servicing. Thanks to awareness campaigns carried out by consumer protection organizations as well as the Ministry of Consumer Protection, Mauritian consumers are becoming more and more concerned about quality and after-sales service.

Protecting Your Intellectual Property Return to top

Intellectual property rights are protected by two pieces of legislation, the new Copyrights Act of 2014 and the Patents, Industrial Designs and Trade Marks Act of 2002. Both pieces of legislation are in line with international norms. Mauritius is a member of the World Intellectual Property Organization (WIPO) and party to the Paris and Bern Conventions for the protection of industrial property and the Universal Copyright Convention.

The Mauritian Police Department would normally take action against IPR infringements only in cases where the IPR owner has an official representative in Mauritius because the Court would require a representative to testify that the products seized are counterfeit. Moreover, the Customs Department of the Mauritius Revenue Authority can intercept the entry of goods suspected of being counterfeits if the trademark owner has undertaken prior registration procedures with the Customs Department. Application forms for registration can be downloaded from the Mauritius Revenue Authority/Customs' website: http://www.mra.gov.mu.

More IPR information is provided in Chapter 6: Investment Climate.

Several general principles are important for effective management of intellectual property ("IP") rights in Mauritius. First, it is important to have an overall strategy to protect your IP. Second, IP is protected differently in Mauritius than in the U.S. Third, rights must be registered and enforced in Mauritius, under local laws. Your U.S. trademark and patent registrations will not protect you in Mauritius. There is no such thing as an "international copyright" that will automatically protect an author's writings throughout the entire world. Protection against unauthorized use in a particular country depends, basically, on the national laws of that country. However, most countries do offer copyright protection to foreign works under certain conditions, and these conditions have been greatly simplified by international copyright treaties and conventions.

Registration of patents and trademarks is on a first-in-time, first-in-right basis, so you should consider applying for trademark and patent protection even before selling your products or services in the Mauritius market. It is vital that companies understand that intellectual property is primarily a private right and that the U.S. government generally cannot enforce rights for private individuals in Mauritius. It is the responsibility of the rights' holders to register, protect, and enforce their rights where relevant, retaining their own counsel and advisors. Companies may wish to seek advice from local attorneys or IP consultants who are experts in Mauritius law. The U.S. Commercial Service can provide a list of local lawyers upon request. The list is also available on our website at http://mauritius.usembassy.gov/public_services.html.

While the U.S. government stands ready to assist, there is little we can do if the rights holders have not taken these fundamental steps necessary to securing and enforcing their IP in a timely fashion. Moreover, in many countries, rights holders who delay enforcing their rights on a mistaken belief that the USG can provide a political resolution to a legal problem may find that their rights have been eroded or abrogated due to legal doctrines such as statutes of limitations, laches, estoppel, or unreasonable delay in prosecuting a law suit. In no instance should U.S. government advice be seen as a substitute for the obligation of a rights holder to promptly pursue its case.

It is always advisable to conduct due diligence on potential partners. Negotiate from the position of your partner and give your partner clear incentives to honor the contract. A good partner is an important ally in protecting IP rights. Consider carefully, however, whether to permit your partner to register your IP rights on your behalf. Doing so may create a risk that your partner will list itself as the IP owner and fail to transfer the rights should the partnership end. Keep an eye on your cost structure and reduce the margins (and the incentive) of would-be bad actors. Projects and sales in Mauritius require constant attention. Work with legal counsel familiar with Mauritius laws to create a solid contract that includes non-compete clauses, and confidentiality/non-disclosure provisions.

It is also recommended that small and medium-size companies understand the importance of working together with trade associations and organizations to support efforts to protect IP and stop counterfeiting. There are a number of these organizations, both Mauritius or U.S.-based. These include:

- The U.S. Chamber and local American Chambers of Commerce
- National Association of Manufacturers (NAM)
- International Intellectual Property Alliance (IIPA)
- International Trademark Association (INTA)
- The Coalition Against Counterfeiting and Piracy
- International Anti-Counterfeiting Coalition (IACC)
- Pharmaceutical Research and Manufacturers of America (PhRMA)
- Biotechnology Industry Organization (BIO)

IP Resources

A wealth of information on protecting IP is freely available to U.S. rights holders. Some excellent resources for companies regarding intellectual property include the following:

- For information about patent, trademark, or copyright issues -- including enforcement issues in the U.S. and other countries -- call the STOP! Hotline: **1-866-999-HALT** or register at http://**www.StopFakes.gov**.

- For more information about registering trademarks and patents (both in the U.S. as well as in foreign countries), contact the U.S. Patent and Trademark Office (USPTO) at: **1-800-786-9199**.

- For more information about registering for copyright protection in the U.S., contact the U.S. Copyright Office at: **1-202-707-5959**.

- For more information about how to evaluate, protect, and enforce intellectual property rights and how these rights may be important for businesses, a free online training program is available at http://www.stopfakes.gov.

- For information on obtaining and enforcing intellectual property rights and market-specific IP Toolkits visit: http://www.stopfakes.gov. This site is linked to the USPTO website for registering trademarks and patents (both in the U.S. as well as in foreign countries), the U.S. Customs & Border Protection website to record registered trademarks and copyrighted works (to assist customs in blocking imports of IP-infringing products) and allows you to register for Webinars on protecting IP.

- The U.S. Commerce Department has positioned IP attachés in key markets around the world. You can get contact information for the IP attaché who covers Mauritius at: Johannesburg.office.box@mail.doc.gov

Information on Mauritian rules and registration procedures for patents, trademarks, and copyrights can be obtained from:

Industrial Property Office (for patents and trademarks)
7th Floor Moorgate House

Sir William Newton Street
Port Louis
Tel: +230 208-5714; Fax: +230 210-9702
Email: trademark@intnet.mu
Website: http://foreign.gov.mu

Copyright Desk (for copyrights)
Ministry of Arts and Culture
Renganaden Seeneevassen Building
Port Louis, Mauritius
Email: spboodhun@mail.gov.mu
Website: http://culture.gov.mu

Mauritius Society of Authors (for copyrights)
Avenue des Artistes
Beau Bassin, Mauritius
Tel: +230 454-7931; Fax: +230 454-0578
Email: copyrightsoc@intnet.mu

Due Diligence   Return to top

The Embassy recommends due diligence before entering into any type of business deal
with local companies. The Embassy's Economic/Commercial Section can provide
valuable background information on Mauritian firms through its International Company
Profile (ICP) service. Further information can be obtained by visiting our website at
http://www.mauritius.usembassy.gov or by contacting your local U.S. Export Assistance
Center or the U.S. Commercial Service in Johannesburg at
http://www.buyusa.gov/southafrica.

Local Professional Services   Return to top

A number of the international accounting and management-consulting firms such as
PriceWaterhouseCoopers, KPMG, Deloitte, BDO, and Ernst and Young are represented
in Mauritius. They provide a range of professional services including audit, tax,
consulting, and financial advisory services.

A list of local attorneys is available on the Embassy website as follows:
http://mauritius.usembassy.gov/barristers.html. The Embassy's Economic/Commercial
Section can be contacted via email at: jathoonisx@state.gov or caunhyerx@state.gov;
Phone: +230 202-4464 or +230 202-4430; Fax: +230 208-9534 or through our website
http://mauritius.usembassy.gov.

For more specific information, please contact:
Mauritius Bar Association
Max City Building (4th Floor)
21 Pope Hennessy Street
Port Louis, Mauritius
Tel: +230 213-9130; Fax: +230 208-8351

Email: mbarcouncil@yahoo.com
Website: http://www.barmauritius.com

Web Resources   Return to top

L'Express (daily) http://www.lexpress.mu

Le Mauricien (daily) http://www.lemauricien.com

Le Matinal (daily) http://www.lematinal.com

Le Defi Quotidien http://www.ledefimedia.info

Week-end (weekly) http://www.week-end.mu

Industrial Property Office http://www.foreign.gov.mu

Copyright Desk, Ministry of Arts and Culture http://culture.gov.mu

Mauritius Network Services http://mns.mu/cbris-companies.php

Public Procurement Office http://www.gov.mu/portal/goc/pposite/file/pporeg.pdf

Government of Mauritius portal http://www.gov.mu/portal/sites/eprocurement/index.jsp

Mauritius Revenue Authority/Customs http://www.mra.gov.mu

U.S. Embassy Port Louis http://www.mauritius.usembassy.gov

U.S. Commercial Service Johannesburg http://www.buyusa.gov/southafrica

Mauritius Bar Association http://www.barmauritius.com

List of local attorneys http://mauritius.usembassy.gov/barristers.html

U.S. patent, trademark and copyright http://www.stopfakes.gov

Registration for USDOC's "SME IP Advisory Program":
http://www.abanet.org/intlaw/intlproj/iprprogram_consultation.html

Return to table of contents

Return to table of contents

Chapter 4: Leading Sectors for U.S. Export and Investment

Commercial Sectors

- Renewable Energy
- Medical Equipment
- Drugs/Pharmaceuticals
- Refrigeration Equipment
- Safety/Security Equipment
- Port Equipment/Port Development

Agricultural Sectors

- Wheat Crude
- Vegetable Oil
- Corn and Soya Bean for Animal Feed

RENEWABLE ENERGY

Overview Return to top

Unit: USD thousands

	2012	2013	2014 (estimated)	2015 (estimated)
Total Market Size	8,850	7,025	7,775	8,650
Total Local Production				
Total Exports				
Total Imports	8,850	7,025	7,775	8,650
Imports from the U.S.		113	120	130
Exchange Rate: 1 USD	30.50	31.00	31.00	31.00

Data Sources: All figures above are from Statistics Mauritius, except for 2014 and 2015 which are Embassy estimates.

The Government of Mauritius' energy policy is to encourage the use of renewable and clean energy in order to reduce the country's dependence on fossil fuels and decrease greenhouse gas emissions through the setting up of wind farms, hydropower stations, the use of landfill gas for energy production, and the optimum utilization of solar energy. The GOM hopes to increase self-sufficiency in terms of electricity supply through use of renewable sources of energy from the current 20 percent to 35 percent by 2025.

A Maurice Ile Durable (Sustainable Island) Fund was created by the GOM in July 2008 and has since financed various programs to promote energy efficiency and savings, including the sale of one million compact fluorescent lamps at a subsidized price to domestic consumers and a grant of USD 330 to 29,000 households for the purchase of solar water heaters. Additionally, the GOM in 2011 drafted a Master Plan for Renewable Energy outlining renewable energy projects through the year 2025 (http://publicutilities.gov.mu).

The GOM is undertaking legal and institutional reforms in the energy sector and plans to establish an independent utility regulatory body to regulate the sector. An Energy Efficiency Act was adopted by parliament in 2011 to provide the framework for product labeling and importation of energy efficient equipment. The GOM also passed a Building Control Act in 2011 to improve building design and choice of building plant and equipment to attain high efficiency in terms of energy use.

The Central Electricity Board (CEB), the public utility body of Mauritius, is the sole agency for transmission, distribution, and sale of electricity in Mauritius. CEB currently produces about 40 percent of the country's total power requirements from four thermal power stations and eight hydroelectric plants. The remaining 60 percent is purchased from Independent Power Producers, mainly private generators from the sugar industry, who produce electricity from bagasse (sugarcane waste) and coal.

Sub-Sector Best Prospects   Return to top

- Wind turbines and wind energy technology
- Compact fluorescent lamps
- Solar energy technology for solar water heaters
- Photovoltaic energy technology
- Power plant based on liquid natural gas technology
- Geothermal energy technology
- Biomass technology
- Waste-to-energy plant for burning solid waste
- Pumping of cold sea water for air conditioning
- Green building design services and equipment

Opportunities   Return to top

In recent years, the GOM has created a solid framework of incentives to move Mauritius towards a diverse energy sector that includes fossil fuels, renewable energy, biomass and energy efficiency projects. U.S. companies will find many opportunities for investing in the renewable and clean energy sector. There are a number of wind and solar power projects under way or operational as well as a Sea Water Air Conditioning (SWAC) project in downtown Port Louis. The GOM has signed renewable energy agreements with the private sector worth USD 277 million since 2011.

Solar Technology: In February 2014, Mauritian firm Sarako, in joint venture with German firm Tauber Solar, completed a 15-megawatt photovoltaic solar farm which is now producing and selling electricity to the Central Electricity Board (CEB), the local power utility. Also, in early 2014, U.S. firm Synnove Energy signed an Energy Supply and Purchase Agreement (ESPA) with the CEB for two photovoltaic solar power plants with a total capacity of 4 megawatts. Earlier, the CEB signed another agreement for a similar capacity solar farm with Astonfield/Alteo, an Indian-Mauritian joint venture. All these renewable energy projects are expected to be completed in 2015. The GOM is willing to consider proposals for more and larger solar PV farms, including unsolicited bids.

Wind Farms: French firm Aerowatt signed an ESPA with the CEB for a 9-megawatt wind farm in the north of the island while Suzlon/PAD, an Indian-Mauritian joint venture, signed another ESPA for an 18-megawatt wind farm in the center of the island. The GOM's Board of Investment is also considering several offshore wind farm projects proposed by foreign companies.

Biomass: In line with its Green Economy policy, the Minister of Finance announced in his 2014 Budget Speech that a Biomass Development Program will be introduced to encourage and give incentives to small planters to grow plants that will be efficient sources of biomass energy. A cooperative of small planters plans to produce biomass energy on 6,000 hectares of marginal land by using the "Arundo Donax" plant. According to the research done locally, this plant can be planted/harvested all year round and can offer a substitute for coal.

Liquid Natural Gas (LNG): The CEB has also commissioned a feasibility study on the use of Liquefied Natural Gas (LNG) for future generating plants. The South African firm carrying out the study is expected to submit its report in mid-2014. The CEB plans the use of LNG both for energy generation and transportation.

Geothermal: A preliminary study on the geothermal potential of Mauritius has been carried out in 2011, funded by the French aid agency, Agence Française de Development. The CEB is currently carrying out some drilling work to look at the potential for geothermal energy before carrying out a full fledge feasibility study.

Deep Ocean Water Application (DOWA) Project: The GOM's Board of Investment is actively promoting the Deep Ocean Water Application (DOWA) project, which consists of pumping cold sea water from a deep ocean current onto the island for the air conditioning of buildings and other applications. Sotravic Ltd, a private local engineering and construction firm, has obtained approval from the GOM to implement such a Sea Water Air Conditioning (SWAC) project in the capital city of Port Louis. Sotravic plans to float an international request for proposals in mid-2014 for the marine and offshore works (laying of undersea pipes, anchor, and pumping connections) in connection with its SWAC project. Given U.S. experience in this type of project, Sotravic is particularly interested in U.S. participation in the upcoming tender. Subsequent phases of the project will involve other water-based activities such as aquaculture, bottled water, and bio-medical products.

Partnering with Mauritian Firms in Africa: Several Mauritian firms are currently involved in or investigating renewable energy projects, particularly hydropower and PV solar farms, in Kenya, Rwanda, Burundi, Madagascar, and Ghana. U.S firms could partner with Mauritian companies to implement energy projects on mainland Africa with the support of Overseas Private Investment Corporation (OPIC), Ex-Im Bank, and the U.S. Trade and Development Agency.

Green Building: The Building Control Act provides opportunities for consultancy services in the design of green buildings and the supply of related equipment and materials. Energy efficiency is now one of the main criteria in the design of public buildings and in rental of private buildings.

Best Practices

The use of a local partner in implementing a project in Mauritius is strongly recommended. The GOM offers two avenues for foreign (including U.S.) firms to enter the Mauritian energy market, either through a tender issued by the Central Electricity Board or by liaising directly with the Board of Investment (the GOM's investment agency), which would vet the project and then assist in coordination with CEB. U.S. firms should consider funding support from U.S. government development finance institutions such as the Overseas Private Investment Corporation, Ex-Im Bank, and the U.S. Trade and Development Agency. The Embassy can assist U.S. firms in identifying a local partner though our International Partner Search or Gold Key Service. Interested parties must apply through the U.S. Commercial Service at the American Consulate in Johannesburg, South Africa. For additional information, please visit our Embassy website at http://mauritius.usembassy.gov or the U.S. Commercial Service Southern Africa site http://www.buyusa.gov/southafrica/en/servicestouscompanies.html.

Contact Information for Key Government and Regulatory Agencies for Energy:

Mr. Somduth Nemchand
Acting Permanent Secretary
Ministry of Energy and Public Utilities
Air Mauritius Center
Port Louis, Mauritius
Tel: +230 405 6705; Fax: +230 210-7408
Email: snemchand@mail.gov.mu
Secretary: akhodabacchas@mail.gov.mu
Website: http://publicutilities.gov.mu

Mr. Shiam Thannoo
General Manager
Central Electricity Board
Royal Road
Curepipe, Mauritius
Tel: +230 601-1100;
Fax: +230 675-7958
E-mail: shiam.thannoo@ceb.intnet.mu
Secretary: Ms. Kursline Lamy: Email: kursline.lamy@ceb.intnet.mu
Website: http://www.ceb.intnet.mu

Mr. Radhamohun Mungur
Director
Energy Efficiency Management Office
8th Floor, C & R Court
49A Labourdonnais Street
Port Louis, Mauritius
Tel: +230 210-7143; Fax: +230 2106978
Email: eemo@mail.gov.mu
Website: http://eemo.gov.mu

Mr. Ken Poonoosamy
Managing Director
Board of Investment
One Cathedral Square
Port Louis, Mauritius
Tel: +230 203-3806; Fax: +230 210-8660
E-mail: ken@investmauritius.com
Website: http://www.investmauritius.com

Web Resources Return to top

Ministry of Energy & Public Utilities: http://publicutilities.gov.mu
Central Electricity Board: http://www.ceb.intnet.mu
Energy Efficiency Management Office: http://eemo.gov.mu
Board of Investment: http://www.investmauritius.com
U.S. Commercial service, Johannesburg, South Africa:
http://www.buyusa.gov/southafrica/en/servicestouscompanies.html

The Embassy's Economic/Commercial Section in Port Louis, Mauritius can be contacted via email at: jathoonisx@state.gov or caunhyerx@state.gov; Phone: +230 202-4464 or +230 202-4430; Fax: +230 208-9534 or visit our website http://mauritius.usembassy.gov.

MEDICAL EQUIPMENT

Overview Return to top

Unit: USD thousands

	2012	2013	2014 (estimated)	2015 (estimated)
Total Market Size	21,300	20,500	22,000	23,500
Total Local Production	25,000	25,500	26,000	26,500
Total Exports	27,300	29,500	30,000	30,500
Total Imports	23,600	24,500	26,000	27,500
Imports from the U.S.	3,500	1,800	2,000	2,200
Exchange Rate: 1 USD	30.50	31.00	31.00	31.00

Data Sources: All figures above are from Mauritius Statistics, except for 2014 and 2015, which are Embassy estimates.

Mauritius' healthcare infrastructure includes

- 5 major public hospitals
- 6 specialized public hospitals
- 17 private multi-specialty clinics
- 11 private specialized clinics
- 29 medical laboratories

Medical and general equipment: Major government-owned hospitals and health clinics are being upgraded and the GOM issues tenders on a regular basis for medical and general equipment for these institutions.

Pharmaceuticals, medical drugs and disposables: Tenders for the procurement of pharmaceutical products, drugs and disposables are normally launched on an annual basis.

New specialized hospitals: In its 2010-2015 Program, the GOM announced plans to build the following specialized hospitals/health care institutions in Mauritius. An Expression of Interest for consultancy services for a feasibility study has already been issued by the GOM for most of the projects.

- An Institute for Women's health
- A National Geriatric Hospital
- A National Pediatric Hospital
- A Regional Institute of Cardiology
- A state-of-the-art National Health Laboratory Services Center
- A National E-Health Strategic Plan to help streamline and enhance health services in the country

In its FY 2014 Budget, the government provided USD 20 million for the setting up of six state of the art operating theaters, three medical clinics, and three community health centers.

Sub-Sector Best Prospects   Return to top

The implementation of the above-mentioned specialized hospitals represents business opportunities for consultancy services for design and construction as well as supply of medical devices, equipment, and pharmaceuticals.

The Ministry of Health issues tenders for its pharmaceutical requirement on an annual basis. Tenders for medical disposables and equipment, however, are issued as and when required during the year. The procurement notices can be accessed from the following Government of Mauritius' Public Procurement Portal: http://publicprocurement.gov.mu/Pages/default.aspx. These leads are transmitted by the Embassy to the U.S. Commercial Service. The best prospects for sale of U.S. medical equipment to both government and private hospitals in the near future include:

- Magnetic Resonance Imaging apparatus
- X-ray apparatus
- Radio therapy bunker
- Operating theater equipment/instruments
- Artificial parts/joints of the body
- Dental surgery and dento-facial orthopedics
- Consultancy services and equipment for specialized diabetes research and treatment centers

- Consultancy services and equipment for specialized centers for elderly care and rehabilitative medicine
- Wellness centers and health resorts
- Healthcare IT solutions to computerize health records

Opportunities Return to top

Mauritius has a strong foundation in healthcare, medical travel, wellness, alternative medicine, medical devices, and medical education.

Over the past few years, Mauritius has experienced sustained growth in the life sciences sector. This sector has significant opportunities in areas of pharmaceutical manufacturing, medical devices, clinical research, agri-biotech and marine biotech.

Two Indian pharmaceutical companies are currently manufacturing antibiotics, anti-cholesterols, anti-malarials, antipyretics and analgesics for export to Africa and elsewhere. Regarding medical devices, five foreign companies (including Johnson & Johnson) are involved in the manufacture of silicone implants, medical disposables, diagnostic kits, orthopedic devices, prosthetic devices, surgical equipment and electrotherapeutic devices. More than 1,000 clinical trials have thus far been carried out on cosmetic and pharmaceutical products. There are also opportunities for activities in plant and marine biotechnology. Mauritian natural flora reportedly includes 634 medicinal plants, of which less than 10 percent have been formally studied thus far. Also, Mauritius' Exclusive Economic Zone of more than 2 million square kilometers provides enormous untapped marine resources.

Two major Indian healthcare providers (Apollo and Fortis) invested in two large private clinics in 2009 in joint ventures with Mauritian partners. In 2010, another Indian venture, Orbit Healthcare Services, invested in a private eye hospital to serve the growing number of foreign patients who are coming to Mauritius for treatment. Furthermore, the Gulf Medical Hospital from the United Arab Emirates plans to invest USD 10 million in a new 80-bed clinic in Mauritius.

Medical tourism is a growing economic sector in Mauritius. The number of foreign patients coming to Mauritius for treatment grew eight-fold in the past four years. The objective of the government is to reach 100,000 patients by 2015. More and more foreign patients are choosing Mauritius for treatment in specialty areas such as ophthalmology, plastic and cosmetic surgery, cardiology and cardio-thoracic surgery.

Medical education is another area with high growth potential. The government's objective is to have five leading medical schools graduating 500 doctors on an annual basis. Several Indian universities have opened branches in Mauritius for medical and dental studies. In May 2013, the University of Geneva signed a Memorandum of Understanding to collaborate with the University of Mauritius in the running of its 6-year medical undergraduate program.

The medical knowledge process outsourcing sector, which includes such activities as medical transcription, medical image processing, and medical claims management currently involves 10 companies employing 500 people. The government's target is to create 1,000 more jobs with 20 more companies operating in this sector by 2015.

Web Resources

Return to top

Ministry of Health and Quality of Life - Website: http://www.health.gov.mu

GOM's Public Procurement Portal: http://publicprocurement.gov.mu/Pages/default.aspx

Board of Investment - Website: http://www.investmauritius.com

The Embassy's Economic/Commercial Section in Port Louis, Mauritius can be contacted via email at: jathoonisx@state.gov or caunhyerx@state.gov; Phone: +230 202-4464 or +230 202-4430; Fax: +230 208-9534 or visit our website http://mauritius.usembassy.gov.

DRUGS/PHARMACEUTICALS

Overview

Return to top

Unit: USD thousands

	2012	2013	2014 (estimated)	2015 (estimated)
Total Market Size	97,000	82,000	89,200	93,300
Total Local Production	3,500	4,000	4,200	4,300
Total Exports	27,500	29,000	30,000	31,000
Total Imports	121,000	107,000	115,000	120,000
Imports from the U.S.	1,400	1,770	1,850	1,900
Exchange Rate: 1 USD	30.50	31.00	31.00	31.00

Data Sources: All figures above are from Statistics Mauritius, except for 2014 and 2015 which are Embassy estimates.

There are 275 private drugstores and 30 wholesalers of pharmaceuticals in Mauritius. Pharmaceutical products can only be imported by wholesalers licensed by the Pharmacy Board of the Ministry of Health.

Mauritius imported USD 107 million of pharmaceuticals in 2013, one third of which was by the Ministry of Health and the other two thirds by the private sector. The government purchases mostly generic medicine by annual tenders issued in July. The private hospitals and drug stores buy mainly branded products through local wholesalers.

India is the main supplier of pharmaceuticals, with 30 percent of the market, followed by France, Switzerland, U.K., and Germany. Imports from the United States in 2013 were at 1.6 percent of total imports; however some European imports originate from U.S. subsidiaries.

Sub-Sector Best Prospects

Return to top

The main categories of pharmaceutical products imported regularly by Mauritius are:

- Medicine not containing antibiotics
- Antibiotics
- Vaccines (human and veterinarian)
- Penicillin
- Insulin
- Blood reagents

Opportunities Return to top

There are opportunities for manufacturing of pharmaceuticals in Mauritius, and for targeting the larger mainland African market. There are currently two pharmaceutical manufacturing companies in Mauritius, namely Mascareigne Pharmaceutical Manufacturing (MPM) and Ajanta (from India). They produce antibiotics, anti-cholesterols, anti-malarials, antipyretics, and painkillers. Ajanta exports the major part of its production to Africa. MPM operates as a subsidary of Parenteral Drug (India) Ltd since 2010, when the latter bought majority stake (USD 15 million) in the company.

Web Resources Return to top

Board of Investment, 16 Jules Koenig Street, Port Louis, Mauritius
Tel: +230 203-3800; Fax: +230 208-2924 Email: Email: contact@investmauritius.com;

Website: http://www.investmauritius.com

Pharmaceutical Association of Mauritius (Mr. Jayesh Rampadarath, President), c/o Trident Health Care Ltd., 2A Falcon Street, Port Louis, Mauritius. Tel: +230 204-7177. Email: jrampadarath@trident.mu

The Embassy's Economic/Commercial Section in Port Louis, Mauritius can be contacted via email at: jathoonisx@state.gov or caunhyerx@state.gov; Phone: +230 202 4464 or +230 202-4430; Fax: +230 208-9534 or visit our website http://mauritius.usembassy.gov.

REFRIGERATION

Overview Return to top

Unit: USD thousands

	2012	2013	2014 (estimated)	2015 (estimated)
Total Market Size	30,060	30,530	31,300	32,250
Total Local Production				
Total Exports	490	670	700	750
Total Imports	30,550	31,200	32,000	33,000
Imports from the U.S.	83	40	45	50
Exchange Rate: 1 USD	30.50	31.00	31.00	31.00

Data Sources: All figures for the indicators below are from Statistics Mauritius, except for 2014 and 2015 which are Embassy estimates

Moving fresh product, including fruits, vegetables, dairy, meat, poultry, and fish from the farm and ocean to the plate of consumers in as high-quality condition as possible is increasingly recognized in Mauritius as important from both the standpoint of customer satisfaction and consumer safety. As incomes rise, more and more fresh or frozen products, which require a continuous stable temperature from their point of production to the consumer's plate, are arriving in the market. As a result, imports of cold chain products, including cold storage equipment, refrigerated trucks and containers, and refrigerated display cases, have been increasing steadily over the past few years. The majority of the cold chain products in Mauritius are currently being imported from France, England, Italy, South Africa, Malaysia, and China.

Sub-Sector Best Prospects Return to top

The best prospects in the cold chain sector include:

- Cold storage equipment
- Refrigerated trucks and containers
- Refrigerated display cases
- Cold chain training program

Opportunities Return to top

In the past four years, the seafood sector witnessed dramatic expansion and has thus emerged as one of the pillars on the Mauritian economy. In 2013 the seafood sector had a turnover of USD 720 million, representing 18 percent of national exports and 1.5 percent of GDP. The Indian Ocean holds the second largest stock of tuna. The seafood sector offers business opportunities in:

- Fishing
- Transshipment
- Storage and warehousing
- Light processing such as grading, cleaning, filleting, loining, and canning

The port and Freeport (free trade zone) offer logistics services and infrastructure facilities for the transshipment of fish in Mauritius. The Mauritius Freeport offers more than 80,000 cubic meters of cold room facilities under controlled temperature from -14 degrees celsius to 28 degrees celsius, built according to international standards. Continued developments in the seafood sector will generate an increasing demand for cold chain equipment and services as well as fish processing equipment.

Web Resources Return to top

The Embassy's Economic/Commercial Section in Port Louis, Mauritius can be contacted via email at: jathoonisx@state.gov or caunhyerx@state.gov; Phone: +230 202-4464 or +230 202-4430; Fax: +230 208-9534 or visit our website http://mauritius.usembassy.gov.

SAFETY/SECURITY EQUIPMENT

Overview

Return to top

Unit: USD thousands

	2012	2013	2014 (estimated)	2015 (estimated)
Total Market Size	11,475	12,500	13,000	13,500
Total Local Production				
Total Exports				
Total Imports	11,475	12,500	13,000	13,500
Imports from the U.S.	1,000	2,000	2,250	2,500
Exchange Rate: 1 USD	30.50	31.00	31.00	31.00

Data Sources: All figures above are from Statistics Mauritius, except for 2014 and 2015 which are Embassy estimates.

Public concerns over the level of crime in Mauritius have been rising steadily in the past few years and as a result, there is an increasing demand for security services. Protecting property and assets is becoming increasingly relevant. Tourism is one of the major pillars of the Mauritian economy and the government's objective is to safeguard the reputation of Mauritius as a safe tourist destination. The government is installing Closed Circuit Television Surveillance Systems in major tourist zones as well as the major cities and has plans to extend the network to other high-risk areas.

Sub-Sector Best Prospects

Return to top

The best prospects in this sector include:

- CCTV, integrated surveillance systems
- Alarm and intruder detection
- Access control systems
- Security locks and digital safe for hotel rooms
- ID management
- Biometrics
- Security services

Opportunities

Return to top

Between 2009 and 2012, close to 225 street surveillance cameras were installed by the authorities in Flic en Flac and Grand Baie, two popular tourist areas while 370 others are currently being placed in the capital city of Port Louis and Quatre Bornes. The government will extend the network to other regions, particularly high-risk areas.

Mauritius has seen a remarkable growth in property development in the past few years with the Integrated Resort Scheme (luxury villas integrated with commercial, sports and wellness facilities), the construction of new hotels, the Ebene cyber city, several large super markets, and shopping malls. These projects are ongoing and all these buildings require security equipment and services, including CCTV and security alarm systems.

In order to protect the safety of their residents, the government requires all hotels to provide electronic security locks and digital safes in their rooms as well as access control systems in secured areas.

Prison security has become a priority for the authorities following several cases of drug trafficking and other incidents involving prisoners. This is generating further demand for security and surveillance equipment.

Web Resources   Return to top

The Embassy's Economic/Commercial Section in Port Louis, Mauritius can be contacted via email at: jathoonisx@state.gov or caunhyerx@state.gov; Phone: +230 202-4464 or +230 202-4430; Fax: +230 208-9534 or visit our website http://mauritius.usembassy.gov.

PORT HANDLING EQUIPMENT/PORT DEVELOPMENT

Overview   Return to top

Unit: USD thousands

	2012	2013	2014 (estimated)	2015 (estimated)
Total Market Size	5,500	7,000	7,500	8,000
Total Local Production				
Total Exports				
Total Imports	5,500	7,000	7,500	8,000
Imports from the U.S.		80	90	100
Exchange Rate: 1 USD	30.50	31.00	31.00	31.00

Data Sources: All figures above are from Statistics Mauritius, except for 2014 and 2015 which are Embassy estimates

As the sole maritime gateway of the country, Port Louis harbor plays a vital role in the national economy as it handles about 99 percent of the total volume of external trade and contributes over 2 percent to the country's GDP.

The Mauritius Ports Authority (MPA) is the sole national port authority to regulate and control the port sector. The MPA provides the main port infrastructure together with related facilities and equipment. The Cargo Handling Corporation Ltd is responsible for the management of all port handling operations pertaining to containers and general cargo. CHC handled 622,000 containers in 2013, up from 576,000 in 2012.

Sub-Sector Best Prospects Return to top

- Gantry cranes
- Forklifts
- Loading and unloading machinery

Opportunities Return to top

In 2014 the Cargo Handling Corporation (CHC) Ltd plans to purchase two more gantry cranes and other port equipment, valued at USD 40 million. It already has five such cranes in operation.

The government will invest Rs 3.2 billion (USD 103 million) in port development in 2014 and a further Rs 2.3 billion (USD 74 million) in the next two years on the following projects:

- Extension of the quay at the Mauritius Container Terminal
- Deepening of the navigation channel so as to accommodate 3rd generation container vessels
- Construction of a cruise terminal building
- Upgrading of the Multi-Purpose Terminal

Web Resources Return to top

Mauritius Ports Authority: http://www.mauport.com

Cargo Handling Corporation Ltd: http://www.chcl.mu

Agricultural Sectors Return to top

Mauritius has always been a net food importing country. Due to its limited size, the absence of economies of scale, and the high comparative advantage of sugar cane in agro-climatic, environmental, and economic terms, Mauritius imports all its essential food requirements, including cereals, wheat, rice, pulses, edible oil, meat, dairy products, and spices, mainly from Europe, South Africa, Australia, and India. Corn and soybean for the production of animal feed are also imported, mostly from Argentina. Mauritius imports fruits such as oranges, apples, grapes as well as a fair proportion of its potato, onion, garlic, and ginger needs. Food imports currently account for USD 700 million, equivalent to 18 percent of Mauritius' total import bill.

In 2010, the Government of Mozambique offered 23,500 hectares of land to the Government of Mauritius, subject to Mauritius coming up with viable and sustainable projects. For this purpose, the Government of Mauritius set up the Regional Development Co. Ltd (RDC) to promote regional food security and other regional development projects. Since 2011, RDC has issued at least two requests for proposals from potential investors for agricultural activities and renewable energy projects. The requests for proposals were open to all investors, regardless of nationality or country of registration. Consequently, APA (Mauritius) Ltd, a Mauritian-based company, partnered with two Indian firms to propose a rice plantation project in Mozambique with an initial investment of USD 10 million.

BAI Group, another local company, is seeking a partner for food crop production or other relevant agricultural activities on the land obtained in Mozambique. Interested partners should contact Mr. Moussa I. Rawat, Chairman, Bramer Corporation (a subsidary of BAI), BAI Executive Suite, Royal Road, Curepipe, Mauritius. Tel: +230 602-3328, E-mail: mirawat@bramercorp.com; Web site: http://www.britishamericaninvestment.com/.

In March 2014, the Government of Ghana put 30,000 hectares of agricultural land at the disposal of Mauritian entrepreneurs. A delegation of government officials as well as private entrepreneurs is expected to visit Ghana in the coming months to explore business opportunities there.

Wheat   Return to top

Overview

Mauritius traditionally imports wheat from France and Australia. In 2013, Mauritius imported 163,000 metric tons of wheat valued at USD 65 million. In 2007-08, due to a poor crop in its traditional markets, Mauritius imported about 50,000 metric tons of wheat from the United States for the first time. The satisfaction with the U.S. wheat and the relationship between U.S. Wheat Associates and the local milling company has opened the door for more U.S. wheat to be sold in the future. U.S. exporters would still need to compete with French and Australian wheat, particularly in terms of price and freight availability.

Best Products

Les Moulins de la Concorde, the only flour mill in Mauritius, has shown interest in the following types of U.S. wheat:

- Hard Red Spring
- Hard White

Resources

Mr. Phillipe Lahausse, Managing Director, Les Moulins de la Concorde Ltee (flourmill), Cargo Peninsula, Port Louis, Mauritius. Tel: +230 240-8180; Fax: +230 240-8171; Email: plahausse@food-allied.com. Website: http://www.food-allied.com.

Mark Samson, Regional Vice President For the Middle East, East & North Africa, U.S. Wheat Associates, Inc., Cairo, Egypt; Tel: +2 02 2380 3162; FAX: +2 02 2380 3138; Email: msamson@uswheat.org; website: http://www.uswheat.org

British American Investment Co.Ltd:
http://www.britishamericaninvestment.com/default2.asp

The Embassy's Economic/Commercial Section in Port Louis, Mauritius can be contacted via email at: jathoonisx@state.gov or caunhyerx@state.gov; Phone: +230 202 4464 or +230 202 4430; Fax: +230 208 9534 or visit our website http://mauritius.usembassy.gov.

Crude Vegetable Oil   Return to top

Overview

Mauritius imports 100 percent of its edible oil requirements. There are two refineries for edible oil operating in Mauritius that import crude vegetable oil and supply 90 percent of the market with refined edible oil. The remaining 10 percent is supplied by importers of refined edible oil in containers that are sold directly to super markets.

Best Products

About 70 percent of the crude oil imported consists of soybean oil, the rest includes sunflower and palm olein. The refined edible oil produced by the refineries is a mixture of soybean oil (75 percent) and palm olein (25 percent).

Opportunities

Mauritius traditionally imports its crude vegetable oil from Argentina and Brazil. In 2013, Mauritius imported 35,000 tons of crude vegetable oil, worth USD 43.6 million. The local refineries negotiate their purchase directly with the big producers such as Nidera and Dreyfuss on a cash against documents basis. U.S. suppliers must be able to compete with Argentina and Brazil on price to get a share of the market. Freight availability is also an important factor for the importers.

Resources
Mauritius Oil Refineries Ltd., Quay Road, Port Louis, Mauritius. Tel: +230 206-9800; Fax: +230 240-8320; Email: moroil@intnet.mu; website: http://www.moroil.mu.

The Embassy's Economic/Commercial Section in Port Louis, Mauritius can be contacted via email at: jathoonisx@state.gov or caunhyerx@state.gov; Phone: +230 202 4464 or +230 202 4430; Fax: +230 208 9534 or visit our website http://mauritius.usembassy.gov.

Corn and Soya Bean for Animal Feed   Return to top

Overview

Mauritius also imports 100,000 metric tons of corn and 40,000 metric tons of soybean annually as inputs for its livestock feed factories. The total grain requirement valued at USD 50 million is traditionally imported from Argentina. The two animal feed factories in Mauritius are willing to consider imports from the U.S. if they are able to get competitive deals in terms of freight and price as with Argentina suppliers. U.S. trade associations, such as the U.S. Grain Council, would need to undertake long-term market development efforts with the local animal feed manufacturers.

Resources

Meaders Feeds Ltd., Riche Terre, Mauritius. Tel: +230 249-3860; Fax: +230 248-1837; Email: meaders@intnet.mu; website: http://www.meaders.com.

Livestock Feed Ltd, Les Guibies, Mauritius. Tel; ++230 286 1112; Fax: +230 286 1114; Email: livestockfeed@food-allied.com; website: http://www.lfl.mu

The Embassy's Economic/Commercial Section in Port Louis, Mauritius can be contacted via email at: jathoonisx@state.gov or caunhyerx@state.gov; Phone: +230 202-4464 or +230 202-4430; Fax: +230 208-9534 or visit our website http://mauritius.usembassy.gov.

Return to table of contents

Return to table of contents

Chapter 5: Trade Regulations, Customs and Standards

- Import Tariffs
- Trade Barriers
- Import Requirements and Documentation
- U.S. Export Controls
- Temporary Entry
- Labeling and Marking Requirements
- Prohibited and Restricted Imports
- Customs Regulations and Contact Information
- Standards
- Trade Agreements
- Web Resources

Import Tariffs Return to top

Mauritius operates a relatively streamlined trade regime. Over the past several years, Mauritius has taken steps to liberalize trade by significantly lowering import tariffs over a wide range of products. The tariff rates currently range from 0 to 30 percent, while the number of tariff bands currently stands at five (0, 5, 10, 15, and 30 percent). Customs Duties are normally imposed on the "c.i.f."(cost, insurance, and freight) value of imported goods. Vehicles, petroleum, alcoholic drinks, and cigarettes are subject to excise duties. With some exceptions, goods imported into Mauritius are also subject to a 15 percent Value Added Tax (VAT). The tariff rates for different types of goods are listed in the Customs Tariff Schedule, which is available at:
http://www.mcci.org/documents/trade/SADC-Customs%20Tariff-Amendment.pdf

Trade Barriers Return to top

There is no discrimination against U.S. companies as far as tariff and non-tariff barriers are concerned.

Import Requirements and Documentation Return to top

Importers are required to submit the following documents:

- Bill of lading/airway bill
- Bill of entry
- Invoice
- Packing list
- Insurance certificate (if applicable)
- Certificate of origin (if applicable)
- Other relevant documents/permits which may be required by government agencies (such as health, agriculture, veterinary services)

Exporters are required to submit the following documents:

- Bill of lading
- Bill of entry
- Invoice
- Packing list
- Insurance certificate (if applicable)
- Export permit (if applicable)
- Certificates of origin for exports to the European Union, countries of the Common Market for Eastern and Southern Africa (COMESA), the Southern African Development Community (SADC), and the Indian Ocean Commission (IOC)

Guidelines for the submission of an application for import permits as well as a list of goods subject to import permits are posted at the Ministry of Industry, Commerce and Consumer Protection's web site: http://commerce.gov.mu/English/Publications/Documents/gn193.pdf.

U.S. Export Controls   Return to top

U.S. companies wanting to export controlled items to Mauritius must apply for licenses from the appropriate government agencies in the United States. The Bureau of Industry and Security (BIS) of the U.S. Department of Commerce is responsible for implementing and enforcing the Export Administration Regulations (EAR), which regulate the export and re-export of certain commercial items. The EAR, including the Commerce Control list, can be accessed at http://www.bis.doc.gov/index.php/regulations/export-administration-regulations-ear. A list of U.S. agencies involved in export controls can be found at http://www.bis.doc.gov/index.php/about-bis/resource-links.

Temporary Entry   Return to top

The Mauritius Customs Department may authorize the temporary entry of goods for a period of six months where the importer furnishes adequate security to cover the duty and other taxes (if applicable) which would otherwise be payable. The importer may be exempted from furnishing security if the goods are covered by documents for temporary entry issued under a recognized international convention, such as the Istanbul Convention. The ATA Carnet, an internationally recognized document for the temporary admission of goods, which is governed by the Istanbul Convention, is administered in Mauritius by the Mauritius Chamber of Commerce and Industry. ATA Carnets do not cover perishable goods or goods for processing or repair. Additional information on the ATA Carnet system can be obtained from the Mauritius Chamber of Commerce at the following link: http://www.mcci.org/ata_carnet.aspx.

Labeling and Marking Requirements   Return to top

Labeling and marking requirements are governed by the Legal Metrology Act, which is available at http://commerce.gov.mu/English/Departments/Pages/LEGAL-METROLOGY-SERVICES.aspx.

Prohibited and Restricted Imports Return to top

Prohibited goods include ivory, tortoise shell and other endangered animal products, underwater fishing guns, second-hand motor vehicles parts and accessories, appliances containing chlorofluorocarbons, asbestos fibers, and publications/films/video cassettes of obscene character. A detailed list of prohibited goods is available at http://mra.gov.mu/index.php/importexport-a-others/import/prohited-goods

Restricted/controlled goods, which may be imported subject to an import permit being granted, include syringes, drugs and psychotropic substances, arms and ammunition, and second-hand motor vehicles. A detailed list of restricted imports is available at http://mra.gov.mu/index.php/importexport-a-others/import/controlled-goods.

Customs Regulations and Contact Information Return to top

Customs regulations for Mauritius can be downloaded from: http://mra.gov.mu/index.php/legislations

Contact information for the Mauritius Customs Office: The Director, Mauritius Revenue Authority, Customs, New Customs House, Mer Rouge, Port Louis, Mauritius, phone: +230 202-0500, fax: +230 216-7601, e-mail: customs@mra.mu.

The Embassy's Economic/Commercial Section in Port Louis, Mauritius can be contacted via email at: jathoonisx@state.gov or caunhyerx@state.gov; Phone: +230 202-4464 or +230 202-4430; Fax: +230 208-9534 or visit our website http://mauritius.usembassy.gov.

Standards Return to top

- Overview
- Standards Organizations
- Conformity Assessment
- Product Certification
- Accreditation
- Publication of Technical Regulations
- Labeling and Marking
- Contacts

Overview Return to top

Mauritius is seeking to enhance its competitiveness and, as such, the government is keen on promoting internationally recognized standards. The Mauritius Standards Bureau is the national standards body involved in the development of standards, while the Mauritius Accreditation Service is the sole agency for providing accreditation to certification bodies in Mauritius. Accreditation in Mauritius is a voluntary process.

Standards Organizations Return to top

The Mauritius Standards Bureau is mandated to develop standards, provide metrology, calibration, testing, and quality assurance services to the manufacturing and service sectors. It publishes a work program of its standards development activities in January and July of each year. The website for the Mauritius Standards Bureau is http://msb.intnet.mu/English/Pages/default.aspx.

NIST Notify U.S. Service: Member countries of the World Trade Organization (WTO) are required under the Agreement on Technical Barriers to Trade (TBT Agreement) to report to the WTO all proposed technical regulations that could affect trade with other Member countries. Notify U.S. is a free, web-based e-mail subscription service that offers an opportunity to review and comment on proposed foreign technical regulations that can affect your access to international markets. Register online at http://www.nist.gov/notifyus/.

Conformity Assessment Return to top

The Mauritius Accreditation Service (MAURITAS) is the sole authority in Mauritius for granting accreditation to conformity assessment bodies involved in calibration, testing, inspection, and certification. MAURITAS benchmarks its level of services with international guidelines and standards.

Product Certification Return to top

The Mauritius Standards Bureau (MSB) is currently the sole product certification body in Mauritius. MSB certification enables companies to use the MSB mark for products and processes that meet all the requirements of the relevant Mauritian standard. The license for use of the mark for products and processes is valid for two years (renewable) during which the MSB conducts regular surveillance visits. Mauritius has signed a Mutual Multilateral Recognition Agreement with the International Laboratory Accreditation Cooperation (ILAC) and the International Accreditation Forum (IAF).

Accreditation Return to top

Accreditation in Mauritius is voluntary. A list of accredited entities in Mauritius is available at http://www.mauritas.org/entities.php.

Publication of Technical Regulations Return to top

Draft standards are published in the Government Gazette and a 60-day period is allocated for public comments. The Minister in charge of industry may, by public notice, transform a standard into a technical regulation after consideration of any written objection filed with the Mauritius Standards Bureau. Contact information for the Mauritius Standards Bureau is provided below.

Labeling and Marking Return to top

The Legal Metrology Act provides for standards of measurement for products sold in Mauritius as well as their labeling. In addition, the Legal Metrology (Pre-packed Commodities) Regulations prescribe the labeling and measurement requirements for prepackaged products. The Legal Metrology Services Department, which operates under the Ministry of Industry, Commerce and Consumer Protection, is responsible for the implementation of the legal metrology system in Mauritius. Additional information is available at http://commerce.gov.mu/English/Departments/Pages/LEGAL-METROLOGY-SERVICES.aspx.

Contacts Return to top

Mauritius Standards Bureau, Villa Road, Moka, Mauritius, contact: Acting Director, tel: +230) 433-3648, fax: +230 433-5051, e-mail: msb@intnet.mu

Ministry of Industry, Commerce and Consumer Protection, 8th floor, Air Mauritius Center, Port Louis, Mauritius, contact: The Permanent Secretary, Tel: +230 201-1068, fax: +230 201-3289. Web: http://commerce.gov.mu/English/Departments/Pages/default.aspx.

The Embassy's Economic/Commercial Section in Port Louis, Mauritius can be contacted via email at: jathoonisx@state.gov or caunhyerx@state.gov; Phone: +230 202-4464 or +230 202-4430; Fax: +230 208-9534 or visit our website http://mauritius.usembassy.gov.

Trade Agreements Return to top

The U.S.-Mauritius Trade and Investment Framework Agreement (TIFA), which was signed in September 2006, provides a formal mechanism to address bilateral trade issues and helps to strengthen and expand trade and investment relations between the two countries. The TIFA can be downloaded from http://www.ustr.gov/trade-agreements/trade-investment-framework-agreements.

Mauritius is also eligible for the trade benefits under the African Growth and Opportunity Act (AGOA), which provides for duty free and quota free access to the U.S. market for over 6,000 products from eligible Sub-Saharan African countries. Additional information on the AGOA can be obtained from http://trade.gov/agoa/. Export of apparel from Mauritius to the United States made from fabric imported from any country is duty free under the AGOA Third Country Fabric Provision. This benefit, which was to expire in September 2012, was extended to September 30, 2015.

Web Resources Return to top

Mauritius Standards Bureau: http://msb.intnet.mu/

Mauritius Accreditation Service: http://www.mauritas.org/

Mauritius Revenue Authority: http://mra.gov.mu

Ministry of Industry, Commerce and Consumer Protection: http://industry.gov.mu

Mauritius Chamber of Commerce and Industry: http://www.mcci.org

U.S. Department of Commerce Bureau of Industry and Security: http://bis.doc.gov

U.S. Trade Representative: http://www.ustr.gov

African Growth and Opportunity Act: http://trade.gov/agoa/

The Embassy's Economic/Commercial Section in Port Louis, Mauritius can be contacted via email at: jathoonisx@state.gov or caunhyerx@state.gov; Phone: +230 202-4464 or +230 202-4430; Fax: +230 208-9534 or visit our website http://mauritius.usembassy.gov.

Return to table of contents

Chapter 6: Investment Climate

- Openness to Foreign Investment
- Conversion and Transfer Policies
- Expropriation and Compensation
- Dispute Settlement
- Performance Requirements and Incentives
- Right to Private Ownership and Establishment
- Protection of Property Rights
- Transparency of Regulatory System
- Efficient Capital Markets and Portfolio Investment
- Competition from State Owned Enterprises
- Corporate Social Responsibility
- Political Violence
- Corruption
- Bilateral Investment Agreements
- OPIC and Other Investment Insurance Programs
- Labor
- Foreign-Trade Zones/Free Ports
- Foreign Direct Investment Statistics
- Web Resources

Openness to Foreign Investment   Return to top

Attitude Toward FDI

Mauritius actively seeks and prides itself on being open to foreign investment. According to the World Bank report "Investing Across Borders," Mauritius has one of the world's most open economies to foreign ownership and is one of the highest recipients of FDI per capita. (See section 1.9 Investment Trends.)

Mauritius is among the freest and most business-friendly countries in Africa according to a number of surveys and metrics. The 2014 Index of Economic Freedom, published annually by The Wall Street Journal and The Heritage Foundation, ranks Mauritius as the 8th freest economy in the world and the 1st out of the 48 countries of Sub-Saharan Africa. For the sixth consecutive year, the World Bank's 2014 Doing Business report ranks Mauritius first among African economies (20th worldwide) in terms of overall ease of doing business. The government's stated objective is for Mauritius to consistently rank among the top 15 most investment- and business-friendly locations in the world.

Other Investment Policy Reviews

Mauritius' economy suffered at the turn of the millennium as longstanding trade preferences in textiles and sugar -- the foundation of its growth strategy -- were phased out. In 2006, the government embarked on an economic reform program aimed at opening the economy, facilitating business, improving the investment climate, and mobilizing foreign direct investment and expertise. These reforms had considerable success in accelerating the rate of growth, reducing unemployment, and speeding up the pace of diversification of the economy through the development of new sectors.

Laws/Regulations of FDI

Investment in Mauritius is governed by the Investment Promotion Act of 2000. Investment regulations are consistent with the WTO's Agreement on Trade Related Investment Measures (TRIMS). The Board of Investment (BOI), the government agency for the facilitation and promotion of investment in Mauritius, acts as a one-stop focal agency for the processing of investment proposals. BOI acts as the facilitator for all forms of investment in Mauritius and guides investors through the necessary processes for doing business in the country. Before starting operations, businesses must register with the Registrar of Companies. Regulations governing incorporation are contained in the Companies Act of 2001. After receipt of a certificate of incorporation from the Registrar of Companies, all companies must register their business activities with the BOI to be able to apply for occupation permit and other facilities offered to investors.

Industrial Strategy

Mauritius has realized a remarkable economic transformation from a monoculture economy based on sugar production to a diversified economy based in export-oriented manufacturing, tourism, and financial/business services. In recent years, information and communication technology (business process outsourcing, call centers, software development), hospitality and property development (commercial malls, luxury villas, and international flagship hotels), the seafood and marine industry (aquaculture, fishing, and processing) and the biomedical industry (medical devices, pharmaceutical products, multi-specialty hospitals) have emerged, attracting substantial investment from both local and foreign investors.

The Government of Mauritius actively promotes Mauritius as a gateway for investment into Africa and the Board of Investment has been mandated to support the expansion of Mauritian companies in Africa. About 75 Mauritian businesses have thus far invested in 26 countries, mainly in Africa and south Asia, in a variety of sectors including sugar, textile, healthcare, agro-industry, IT, banking and finance, and renewable energy. There are opportunities for joint ventures between U.S. and Mauritian firms to do business in Africa with assistance from U.S. development finance institutions such as Overseas Private Investment Corporation (OPIC), U.S. Export-Import Bank (Ex-Im Bank), and U.S. Trade and Development Agency (TDA). In April 2014, Embassy Port Louis hosted a workshop where OPIC Regional Director Peter Ballinger explained the financing programs of OPIC, Ex-Im and TDA to Mauritian businesses. The event was attended by more than 50 CEOs, heads of trade groups, and government representatives and generated a lot of interest from local entrepreneurs, especially those who plan to invest in Africa.

Mauritius offers excellent opportunities in the following sectors:

-Ocean Economy: Mauritius's maritime zone is 2.3 million square kilometers, about the size of Western Europe. The Government of Mauritius' Roadmap on the Ocean

Economy (www.oceaneconomy.mu) provides business opportunities in the following clusters:

- Seabed exploration for hydrocarbon and minerals
- Fishing, seafood processing, and aquaculture
- Deep Ocean Water Applications (Two private companies from Mauritius and Japan are investing more than $200 million in two projects that will pump cold sea water from 1 kilometer under the ocean's surface in order to air-condition buildings in Port Louis and Mahebourg.)
- Marine services such as financing, ship registry, tourism, and marine biotech
- Seaport-related activities and improvements
- Marine renewable energies (wind and tidal)
- Ocean knowledge (research, development, innovation)

-Renewable Energy and Environment:

- Solar, wind, tidal farms
- Manufacturing/assembly of renewable energy products
- Energy efficiency projects
- Solid waste management and waste to energy projects
- Water management and desalination of sea water

-Healthcare and Life Sciences:

- The manufacture of medical disposables, surgical instruments, orthopedic devices, electro-medical devices, and implantable devices
- Pharmaceuticals
- Clinical research
- Agricultural biotechnology
- Marine biotechnology

-Information Technology and Business Process Outsourcing:

- Business process outsourcing: non-voice and voice (customer support, technical help-desk, telemarketing, front office management)
- IT outsourcing, data centers, disaster recovery
- Multimedia and design
- Mobile applications development
- Knowledge/legal process outsourcing

-Agro-Industry:

- Seed production for the local and international market
- Production of crops for export
- Processing of fruits and vegetables
- Agro-projects in the regional markets: Companies have set up rice seed, rice and corn cultivation in Mozambique through the Regional Development Company (RDC) of Mauritius initiative. The RDC is an entity set up by the Government of Mauritius to act as the link between Mozambican authorities and prospective investors, and accompany the latter in their implementation phase.

Limits on Foreign Control

The GOM does not discriminate between local and foreign investment, except in television broadcasting, sugar production, and certain activities in the tourism sector. For these regulated activities an application for the appropriate permit or license must be made to the competent authorities prior to start of operations. For such activities, investors should seek advice from the Board of Investment (www.investmauritius.com). Businesses can be conducted locally in several forms: under a self-employed activity, as a partnership with Mauritian nationals, or a 100 percent foreign-owned company under the Companies Act.

Privatization Program

The GOM has no privatization program but has stated that it plans to reform parastatal bodies as recommended by the IMF. Parastatal companies control key utilities including electricity, water, waste water, postal services, and television broadcasting. The government also controls the import of what it deems to be strategic products such as rice (only non-basmati or other non-luxury rice), wheat flour, and petroleum products through the State Trading Corporation.

Screening of FDI

All investment proposals are screened by the Board of Investment, which provides support services and all relevant information to potential investors on any matter relating to investments. BOI acts as the single interface with all investors and liaises with relevant authorities for the granting of work permits, residence permits and other relevant permits required by the investor to operate in Mauritius.

In late 2013, the GOM established a Fast Track Committee under the chairmanship of the Financial Secretary in the Ministry of Finance and Economic Development to expedite the processing of all permits and approvals concerning major investment projects. The Fast Track Committee meets on a monthly basis, convening representatives of various government ministries (depending on the projects under review) and the Prime Minister's Office. The Committee held its first meeting in February 2014.

Competition Law

The Competition Commission of Mauritius (CCM) is a statutory body established in 2009 to enforce the Competition Act 2007. This Act established a competition regime in Mauritius, under which the CCM can investigate possible anticompetitive behavior by businesses. In its investigations, the CCM has considerable powers to compel businesses and others involved to provide evidence in order to prove or disprove allegations. If it decides that a business's conduct is anticompetitive, CCM has strong powers to intervene and correct the situation. Where businesses have been found to be deliberately fixing prices or colluding in the marketplace, the Commission can impose fines. Since it began operations, the Competition Commission has already undertaken 22 investigations, out of which 15 have been completed and 7 are ongoing. The results of completed investigations are available on CCM's website at www.ccm.mu.

Investment Trends

Since the 2006 reforms, Mauritius has attracted about USD 2.4 billion from foreign investors, including USD 443 million in 2010, USD 339 million in 2011, USD 419 million in 2012, and USD 307 in 2013. The main sources of FDI are France, South Africa, the United Kingdom, and the United Arab Emirates.

Recent U.S. investments in Mauritius are in solar energy, tourism/hotel management, business process outsourcing/software development, diamond cutting and polishing, and the manufacture of silicone implants for cosmetic and reconstructive surgery.

French firms have recently invested in a new tuna processing plant and fishing vessels as well as the production of bone substitutes used in orthopedics and dental surgery. South African companies are investing heavily in property development, retail trade, banking, and IT-enabled services. Several Indian and British universities have recently opened branches in Mauritius.

Tables

TABLE 1: The following chart summarizes several well-regarded indices and rankings.

Measure	Year	Rank or value	Website Address
TI Corruption Perceptions index	2013	52 of 177	http://cpi.transparency.org/cpi2013/results/
Heritage Foundation's Economic Freedom index	2014	8 of 185	http://www.heritage.org/index/ranking
World Bank's Doing Business Report "Ease of Doing Business"	2014	20 of 189	http//doingbusiness.org/rankings
Global Innovation Index	2013	59 of 142	http://www.globalinnovationindex.org/content.aspx?page=gii-full-report-2013#pdfopener
World Bank GNI per capita	2012	USD 8,570	http://data.worldbank.org/indicator/NY.GNP.PCAP.CD

Conversion and Transfer Policies   Return to top

Foreign Exchange

The GOM abolished foreign exchange controls in 1994. Consequently, no approval is required for the repatriation of profits, dividends, or capital gains earned by a foreign investor in Mauritius. In general, businesses do not have difficulty obtaining foreign exchange.

The exchange rate is market-determined, but a small number of institutions dominate the market with the Bank of Mauritius, the central bank, occasionally intervening. In March 2014, gross international reserves stood at USD 3.7 billion, representing an import cover of 5.6 months. During the 12 months ending March 2014, the Mauritian rupee appreciated by 2.8 percent against the U.S. dollar but depreciated against the Euro and Pound Sterling by 3.9 percent and 5.8 percent, respectively.

Remittance Policies

There is no restriction on the remittance of profits, dividends, and capital gains earned by a foreign investor in Mauritius. Mauritius has a well-developed and modern banking system. There is good currency convertibility on both capital and current accounts; settlement can be done in foreign currency, and foreign currency accounts can be opened in Mauritius. There is no legal parallel market in Mauritius for investment remittances.

Expropriation and Compensation	Return to top

The Constitution of the Republic of Mauritius includes a guarantee against nationalization. The Government of Mauritius has never nationalized a business entity.

Dispute Settlement	Return to top

Legal System, Specialized Courts, Judicial Independence, Judgments of Foreign Courts

The Mauritian legal system is based on a combination of English common law and French civil law. The domestic legal system is generally non-discriminatory and transparent. Members of the judiciary are independent of the legislature and the government. The highest court of appeal is the judicial committee of the Privy Council of England. Mauritius is a member of the International Court of Justice. A Commercial Court was established in early 2009 to expedite the settlement of commercial disputes.

Bankruptcy

The Insolvency Act of 2009 amended and consolidated the law relating to insolvency of individuals and companies and the distribution of assets on insolvency and related matters. Most notably, the Act introduced administration procedures, providing creditors the option of a more orderly reorganization or restructuring of a business than in liquidation. The Act can be accessed through the Board of Investment's website: www.investmauritius.com.

Investment Disputes

There has never been an expropriation of private assets in Mauritius. Emtel Ltd., a local firm in joint venture with Millicom International Cellular (majority U.S. investors), has been engaged in a lengthy dispute (since 2005) with Mauritius Telecom, its cellular subsidiary Cellplus (now branded as Orange), and the former Telecommunications Authority, over allegations of unfair competitive practices by Mauritius Telecom and Orange. The case remains in the courts.

International Arbitration

The International Arbitration Act of 2009 reduced the likelihood of international dispute cases decided in arbitration to end up in the Mauritian courts system. The Mauritius International Arbitration Center, set up under the Act, is associated with the London Court of International Arbitration. The Mauritius Chamber of Commerce and Industry also maintains an Arbitration and Mediation Center, internationally recognized as an institution for commercial dispute settlement.

ICSID Convention and New York Convention

Mauritius is a member of the International Center for the Settlement of Investment Disputes and the Multilateral Investment Guarantee Agency of the World Bank. Mauritius is also a signatory to the New York Convention.

Duration of Dispute Resolution

The duration of dispute resolution in courts normally varies between five to ten years. The Mauritius International Arbitration Center, established in 2009, resolves an estimated 75% of its cases within one year and the remainder, in most cases, in less than two years. The Mauritius Chamber of Commerce and Industry's Arbitration and Mediation Center sets a maximum of six months for its arbitrators to settle disputes. However, the parties can mutually agree to extend the term of arbitration to account for scheduling and documentation challenges. Most cases brought to the MCCI's Arbitration and Mediation Center are resolved between six months and one year.

Performance Requirements and Incentives   Return to top

WTO/TRIMS

The Mauritian investment code is in line with the WTO's Agreement on Trade Related Investment Measures (TRIMS).

Investment incentives are applied uniformly to both domestic and foreign investors. Mauritius offers a low tax jurisdiction and a number of other fiscal incentives as follows:

- flat corporate and income tax rate of 15 percent
- 100% foreign ownership permitted
- no minimum foreign capital required
- no tax on dividends
- no capital gains tax

- free repatriation of profits, dividends, and capital
- accelerated depreciation on acquisition of plant, machinery and equipment
- exemption from customs duty on equipment
- direct cash incentives for employers recruiting and training young talent
- extensive network of Double Taxation Avoidance treaties (as of April 2014, Mauritius had such treaties with 45 countries).

Additionally, the government has set up the Integrated Resorts Scheme (IRS) to attract high net worth non-citizens desiring to acquire real estate of not less than USD 500,000 in Mauritius (within a resort approved by the Board of Investment) for personal residence. The Real Estate Scheme (RES) introduced in 2007 allows non-citizens to acquire a residence with no minimum price set. The investor and his/her spouse and dependents are granted resident permits to live in Mauritius when a residential property is acquired for a price exceeding USD 500,000. More detailed information on the incentives is available on BOI's website: www.investmauritius.com.

Performance Requirements

A foreign investor, a non-national professional under a contract of employment, or a self-employed non-national may apply for an Occupation Permit, which allows him/her to reside and work in Mauritius. It is both a work and residence permit.

Occupation Permit: An investor, a professional or a self-employed person may be eligible for an occupation permit under the following conditions:

-Investor: the proposed business activity should generate an annual turnover exceeding MUR 4 million (approx. USD 133,000) with an initial investment of USD 100,000.

-Professional: the basic monthly salary should exceed MUR 45,000 (approx. USD 1,500). However, the basic salary for professionals in the Information and communication Technology Sector should exceed MUR 30,000 monthly (approx. USD 1,000).

-Self-Employed: the annual income from the proposed business activity should exceed MUR 600,000 (approx. USD 20,000) annually with an initial investment of USD 35,000.

Professionals who earn more than USD 3,000 per month and investors having made an investment of more that USD 100,000 may acquire real estate (including an apartment in a ground-plus-two floor complex) as from date of issue of their Occupation Permit.

Permanent Residence Permit: An investor may subsequently apply for a Permanent Residence Permit if his/her business activity generates an annual turnover exceeding MUR 15 million (approx. USD 500,000) during the first three years. In the case of self-employed persons, the business activity should generate an annual income exceeding MUR 3 million (approx. USD 100,000). The Permanent Residence Permit (PRP) is valid for 10 years and PRP holders can acquire properties in his/her own name.

Non-citizens having invested a minimum of USD 500,000 in a qualifying business activity will obtain a Permanent Residence Permit with the right to acquire an apartment in a ground-plus-two floor development. The list of qualifying business activities includes:

Agro-based industry, Banking, Construction, Education, Financial Services, Insurance, Fishing and Marine Resources, Freeport, Healthcare, Information Technology, Infrastructure, Real Estate (excluding the acquisition of a residential property), Leisure, Manufacturing, Marina Development, Power Industry, Tourism and Warehousing.

Right to Private Ownership and Establishment   Return to top

Under the Non-Citizens (Property Restriction) Act, a non-citizen investor may acquire property in Mauritius with the prior approval of the Prime Minister. However, the Prime Minister's approval is not required when the property is acquired:

- under a lease agreement not exceeding 20 years,
- under the Integrated Resort Scheme or Real Estate Scheme for the purchase of a villa,
- under the Invest-Hotel Scheme for the acquisition of a hotel room, or
- when the investor has obtained approval from the Board of Investment to acquire property for use in his/her business.

In his Budget Speech in December 2013, the Minister of Finance announced that high net worth individuals who have chosen to retire in Mauritius will now have the right to purchase an apartment upon a minimum transfer of USD 120,000 at the time of application.

Protection of Property Rights   Return to top

Real Property

Property rights are respected. Mauritius maintains a sophisticated and impartial legal system based on both English common law and French civil law. The system protects all tangible property.

Intellectual Property Rights

Intellectual property rights are protected by two pieces of legislation, the new Copyrights Act passed by the National Assembly in April 2014 and the Patents, Industrial Designs and Trade Marks Act of 2002. Both pieces of legislation are in line with international norms. Mauritius is a member of the World Intellectual Property Organization (WIPO) and party to the Paris and Bern Conventions for the protection of industrial property and the Universal Copyright Convention.

The trademark and patent laws comply with the WTO's Trade Related Aspects of Industrial Property Rights (TRIPS) agreement and protect designs, brands, and technological inventions. Also, the law dictates that well-known international trademarks are protected, whether they are registered in Mauritius or not. A trademark is initially registered for 10 years and may be renewed for successive periods of 10 years. A patent is granted for 20 years and cannot be renewed.

The police, customs, and judicial authorities have effectively enforced trademark and copyright protection for firms like Polo Ralph Lauren and legitimate distributors of

Bollywood films that have established a legal or commercial presence in Mauritius. However, U.S. and European producers and distributors of cinema have in general not established any representation in Mauritius, and protection of their copyrights is practically non-existent. According to a leading IPR law firm, the police will only take action against IPR infringements in cases where the IPR owner has an official representative in Mauritius because the courts require a representative to testify that the products seized are counterfeit. The Customs Department also requires right holders or authorized users to register their trademarks and copyrights with its office in order to seize suspicious goods at the ports of Mauritius. Application forms for registration can be downloaded from the Mauritius Revenue Authority/Customs' website: http://mra.gov.mu.

For additional information about treaty obligations and points of contact at local IP offices, please see WIPO's country profiles at http://www.wipo.int/directory/en/.

Embassy point of contact: Patrick Koucheravy, KoucheravyPE@state.gov

Local lawyers list: http://mauritius.usembassy.gov/barristers.html

Transparency of Regulatory System   Return to top

In recent years, the government has brought radical reforms to trade, investment, tariff, and income tax regulations to simplify the framework for doing business. Trade licenses and many other bureaucratic hurdles have been abolished. With a well-developed legal and commercial infrastructure and a tradition of both entrepreneurship and representative government, Mauritius is one of Africa's most successful democracies. Mauritius also has a long-standing tradition of government and private sector dialogue that allows the private sector to effectively voice its views on the development strategy of the country. The Joint Economic Council, the coordinating body of the Mauritian private sector, is a key vehicle in this regard.

Companies in Mauritius are regulated by the Companies Act of 2001, which incorporates international best practices and promotes accountability, openness, and fairness. In order to combat money laundering and terrorist financing, the government also enacted the Prevention of Corruption Act, the Prevention of Terrorism Act, and the Financial Intelligence and Anti-Money Laundering Act.

A Central Procurement Board, established under the Public Procurement Act 2006, oversees all forms of procurement by public bodies. The Procurement Policy Office is responsible for formulating policies and issuing directives for the operation of a transparent and efficient public procurement system. According to the Procurement Act, a bidder or potential bidder can challenge the procurement proceedings of a public body at any stage and request the Chief Executive Officer of the public body to consider his complaint and, where appropriate, take remedial action. Appeals may be brought against the decisions of a Chief Executive Officer to an Independent Review Panel. A simplified two-tier process, therefore, is available to unsatisfied persons to seek remedy.

Efficient Capital Markets and Portfolio Investment   Return to top

With its well-developed financial services sector, Mauritius aims at becoming a regional financial center. According to the IMF, the banking sector is robust and the financial system has proven resilient to external shocks. Recognized as a well-regulated and transparent jurisdiction, Mauritius has successfully established itself as an international center for cross-border investments.

The Stock Exchange of Mauritius (SEM) has performed well in terms of the volume of transactions, the number of listed companies, market capitalization, and the fairness and efficiency of its operations since its launch in 1989. As of the end of March 2014, the Stock Exchange of Mauritius had 42 companies listed on the Official Market and 47 companies on the Development and Enterprise Market, which is designed for small and medium enterprises. Market capitalization grew markedly from USD 92 million in 1989 to USD 7 billion in March 2014. The SEM is a member of the World Federation of Exchanges, which reports that the SEM adheres to industry business standards.

In November 2007, the SEM was included in the new Morgan Stanley Capital International (MSCI) Frontier Market Indices, which are designed to track the performance of a range of equity markets that are now more accessible to global investors. Mauritius was among four countries in Africa to be included in the new indices. The SEM has also been included in the DOW Jones SAFE 100 Index that was launched in March 2009 by the South Asian Federation of Exchanges (SAFE). The DOW Jones SAFE 100 Index measures the performance of the 50 largest stocks trading in India and the 50 largest stocks trading in four other countries, including Mauritius. The SEM's daily data has also been tracked live on Bloomberg since 2008.

The Mauritius stock market was opened to foreign investors following the lifting of the foreign exchange controls in 1994. No approval is required for the trading of shares by foreign investors unless the investment is for the purpose of legal and management control of a Mauritian company or for the holding of more than 15 percent in a sugar company. Incentives to foreign investors include free repatriation of revenue from the sale of shares and exemption from tax on dividends and capital gains.

The Bourse Africa Ltd., formerly known as the Global Board of Trade, the first multi-asset derivatives exchange of its kind in Africa, began operating in Mauritius in October 2010. It offers a basket of commodities and currency derivative products on its electronic exchange platform, including metals, energy, agricultural commodities, and currency futures.

Mauritius has an active global (offshore) business sector, which is a major route for foreign investments into the Asian sub-continent. Mauritius is the largest source of FDI and portfolio investment in India, estimated at USD 77 billion for the period April 2000-December 2013, which accounts for 37 percent of the total FDI inflows into India. Major U.S. corporations use the Mauritius offshore sector to channel their investment to India. A particularly favorable Double Taxation Avoidance Treaty (DTAT) that exists between Mauritius and India is the main attraction for these investments. As of April 2014, Mauritius had DTATs with a total of 45 countries, including China, Malaysia, Singapore, South Africa, U.K, France, Germany, Kuwait, U.A.E., Egypt and Nigeria.

Mauritius has a relatively sophisticated banking sector with 23 banks currently licensed to undertake banking business. The Banking Act of 2004 provides for banking business to be conducted under a single banking license regime. Accordingly, all banks are free to conduct business in all currencies, including the Mauritian rupee. There are also several non-bank financial institutions, which are authorized to conduct deposit-taking business as well as foreign exchange dealers.

The banking system is highly concentrated and dominated by two, long-established domestic groups, Mauritius Commercial Bank (MCB) and State Bank of Mauritius (SBM), that hold a combined 65 percent of all Mauritian banking assets. Foreign banks present in Mauritius include the Hong Kong and Shanghai Banking Corporation (HSBC), Barclays Bank, Bank of Baroda, Habib Bank, Banque des Mascareignes, PT Bank International Indonesia, Deutsche Bank, Standard Bank, Standard Chartered Bank, and Investec Bank.

The banking sector primarily focuses on trade financing and on the provision of working capital. Accounts may be opened in all major currencies as well as the Mauritian rupee (MUR). Several commercial banks offer card-payment services, such as credit and debit cards and direct debits. Other facilities, including phone banking, home banking, and internet banking are also provided by some banks. Commercial banks offer spot and forward transactions in all major currencies.

Commercial banks have diversified into non-banking business through subsidiaries and affiliates. Banks are engaged in the provision of leasing, stock brokering, asset and fund management, investment and private banking business, insurance, and portfolio and custodial management. As of December 2013, commercial banks' total assets amounted to USD 32.6 billion.

The Bank of Mauritius, the country's central bank, carries out the supervision and regulation of banks as well as non-bank financial institutions authorized to accept deposits. An updated Bank of Mauritius Act, which strengthened the central bank's institutional framework as well as its supervisory powers, was enacted in October 2004. It also has the power to establish prudential safety and soundness standards and regulations, and does so primarily by issue of Guidelines/Guidance Notes. The Bank of Mauritius has endorsed the Core Principles for Effective Banking Supervision as set out by the Basel Committee on Banking Supervision. In July 2009, the Bank of Mauritius Act was amended to provide for the setting up of a Financial Stability Committee comprised of the central bank, the Financial Services Commission, and the Ministry of Finance to review, on a regular basis, the soundness of the financial system.

Competition from State Owned Enterprises   Return to top

The government's stated policy is to act as a facilitator to business, leaving production to the private sector. The government, however, still controls key utility services directly or through parastatal companies in the following industries:

- Energy and Mining: power and water utilities
- Media and Entertainment: television broadcasting
- Services: postal services

The government also controls the import of what it deems to be strategic products such as rice (only non-basmati or other non-luxury rice), wheat flour, and petroleum products through the State Trading Corporation. The government has controlling shares in the State Bank of Mauritius, Air Mauritius (the national airline), Mauritius Ports Authority, and Mauritius Telecom. These state-controlled companies have a Board of Directors on which seats are allocated to senior government officials. The government nominates the chairperson of each board.

OECD Guidelines on Corporate Governance of SOEs

Mauritius is a member of the OECD Network on Corporate Governance of State-Owned Enterprises in Southern Africa. The state-owned companies in Mauritius are required by law to publish an annual report and to submit their books to independent audit. They also are subject to the same corporate social responsibility rules as private firms.

Corporate Social Responsibility   Return to top

OECD Guidelines for Multinational Enterprises

Mauritius is not an adherent to the OECD Guidelines for Multinational Enterprises.

The Government of Mauritius has established a Corporate Social Responsibility (CSR) policy whereby all profitable firms (local or foreign-owned) are required to spend two percent of their chargeable income of the preceding year on Government-approved activities/programs that contribute to the socioeconomic and environmental development of Mauritius.

Approved areas of activity include the eradication of poverty, vocational training for vulnerable groups, promotion of human rights, support to the disabled and the elderly, gender issues and women's empowerment, prevention of violence against women, entrepreneurship and small enterprise development, support to vulnerable children and youth, rehabilitation of drug addicts, protection and preservation of the environment, health and nutrition, social housing, leisure and sports, and promotion of arts and crafts. All projects are reviewed by a National Corporate Social Responsibility Committee.

Major corporate groups in Mauritius, in partnership with non-governmental organizations, have implemented a number of CSR projects related to social housing, health, education and training, leisure and sports, environmental protection, and sustainable development. There is greater awareness on the part of private companies of the need to be accountable to the community. Firms that undertake corporate social responsibility projects are viewed favorably.

Political Violence   Return to top

Mauritius has a long tradition of political and social stability. Civil unrest and political violence are uncommon. Inter-ethnic tensions, however, led to four days of rioting in February 1999, following the death of a popular minority singer while he was in police custody. Governments since then have sought to calm ethnic tensions and stress national unity. Free and fair elections are held every five years with the last general elections held on May 5, 2010, which passed without incident.

Corruption, including bribery, raises the costs and risks of doing business. Corruption has a corrosive impact on both market opportunities overseas for U.S. companies and the broader business climate. It also deters international investment, stifles economic growth and development, distorts prices, and undermines the rule of law.

It is important for U.S. companies, irrespective of their size, to assess the business climate in the relevant market in which they will be operating or investing, and to have an effective compliance program or measures to prevent and detect corruption, including foreign bribery. U.S. individuals and firms operating or investing in foreign markets should take the time to become familiar with the relevant anticorruption laws of both the foreign country and the United States in order to properly comply with them, and where appropriate, they should seek the advice of legal counsel.

The U.S. government seeks to level the global playing field for U.S. businesses by encouraging other countries to take steps to criminalize their own companies' acts of corruption, including bribery of foreign public officials, by requiring them to uphold their obligations under relevant international conventions. A U. S. firm that believes a competitor is seeking to use bribery of a foreign public official to secure a contract should bring this to the attention of appropriate U.S. agencies, as noted below.

U.S. Foreign Corrupt Practices Act: In 1977, the United States enacted the Foreign Corrupt Practices Act (FCPA), which makes it unlawful for a U.S. person, and certain foreign issuers of securities, to make a corrupt payment to foreign public officials for the purpose of obtaining or retaining business for or with, or directing business to, any person. The FCPA also applies to foreign firms and persons who take any act in furtherance of such a corrupt payment while in the United States. For more detailed information on the FCPA, see the FCPA Lay-Person's Guide at: http://www.justice.gov/criminal/fraud/.

Other Instruments: It is U.S. government policy to promote good governance, including host country implementation and enforcement of anti-corruption laws and policies pursuant to their obligations under international agreements. Since enactment of the FCPA, the United States has been instrumental to the expansion of the international framework to fight corruption. Several significant components of this framework are the OECD Convention on Combating Bribery of Foreign Public Officials in International Business Transactions (OECD Antibribery Convention), the United Nations Convention against Corruption (UN Convention), the Inter-American Convention against Corruption (OAS Convention), the Council of Europe Criminal and Civil Law Conventions, and a growing list of U.S. free trade agreements.

OECD Antibribery Convention: The OECD Antibribery Convention entered into force in February 1999. As of March 2009, there are 38 parties to the Convention including the United States (see http://www.oecd.org/dataoecd/59/13/40272933.pdf). Major exporters China, India, and Russia are not parties, although the U.S. government strongly endorses their eventual accession to the Convention. The Convention obligates the Parties to criminalize bribery of foreign public officials in the conduct of international business. The United States meets its international obligations under the OECD Antibribery Convention through the U.S. FCPA.

UN Convention: The UN Anticorruption Convention entered into force on December 14, 2005, and there are 158 parties to it as of November 2011 (see http://www.unodc.org/unodc/en/treaties/CAC/signatories.html). The UN Convention is the first global comprehensive international anticorruption agreement. The UN Convention requires countries to establish criminal and other offences to cover a wide range of acts of corruption. The UN Convention goes beyond previous anticorruption instruments, covering a broad range of issues ranging from basic forms of corruption such as bribery and solicitation, embezzlement, trading in influence to the concealment and laundering of the proceeds of corruption. The Convention contains transnational business bribery provisions that are functionally similar to those in the OECD Antibribery Convention and contains provisions on private sector auditing and books and records requirements. Other provisions address matters such as prevention, international cooperation, and asset recovery. Mauritius is a signatory of the UN Anticorruption Convention.

Free Trade Agreements: While it is U.S. government policy to include anticorruption provisions in free trade agreements (FTAs) that it negotiates with its trading partners, the anticorruption provisions have evolved over time. The most recent FTAs negotiated now require trading partners to criminalize "active bribery" of public officials (offering bribes to any public official must be made a criminal offense, both domestically and trans-nationally) as well as domestic "passive bribery" (solicitation of a bribe by a domestic official). All U.S. FTAs may be found at the U.S. Trade Representative Website: http://www.ustr.gov/trade-agreements/free-trade-agreements.

Local Laws: U.S. firms should familiarize themselves with local anticorruption laws, and, where appropriate, seek legal counsel. While the U.S. Department of Commerce cannot provide legal advice on local laws, the Department's U.S. Commercial Service and the U.S. Embassy in Port Louis can provide assistance with navigating the host country's legal system and obtaining a list of local legal counsel.

Assistance for U.S. Businesses: The U.S. Department of Commerce offers several services to aid U.S. businesses seeking to address business-related corruption issues. For example, the U.S. Commercial Service and U.S. Embassy Port Louis can provide services that may assist U.S. companies in conducting their due diligence as part of the company's overarching compliance program when choosing business partners or agents overseas. The U.S. Commercial Service can be reached directly through its offices in every major U.S. and foreign city, or through its Website at www.trade.gov/cs.

The Departments of Commerce and State provide worldwide support for qualified U.S. companies bidding on foreign government contracts through the Commerce Department's Advocacy Center and State's Office of Commercial and Business Affairs. Problems, including alleged corruption by foreign governments or competitors, encountered by U.S. companies in seeking such foreign business opportunities can be brought to the attention of appropriate U.S. government officials, including local embassy personnel and through the Department of Commerce Trade Compliance Center "Report A Trade Barrier" Website at tcc.export.gov/Report_a_Barrier/index.asp.

Guidance on the U.S. FCPA: The Department of Justice's (DOJ) FCPA Opinion Procedure enables U.S. firms and individuals to request a statement of the Justice Department's present enforcement intentions under the anti-bribery provisions of the FCPA regarding any proposed business conduct. The details of the opinion procedure are available on DOJ's Fraud Section Website at www.justice.gov/criminal/fraud/fcpa. Although the Department of Commerce has no enforcement role with respect to the FCPA, it supplies general guidance to U.S. exporters who have questions about the FCPA and about international developments concerning the FCPA. For further information, see the Office of the Chief Counsel for International Counsel, U.S. Department of Commerce, Website, at http://www.ogc.doc.gov/trans_anti_bribery.html. More general information on the FCPA is available at the Websites listed below.

Exporters and investors should be aware that generally all countries prohibit the bribery of their public officials, and prohibit their officials from soliciting bribes under domestic laws. Most countries are required to criminalize such bribery and other acts of corruption by virtue of being parties to various international conventions discussed above.

Mauritius-Specific Information: Mauritius is a signatory member of the UN Anticorruption Convention and was assessed on Chapters 3 and 4 of said Convention in 2012.

Mauritius placed 52nd out of 177 countries in the 2013 Corruption Perceptions Index published by Transparency International. Although Mauritius remains among the least corrupt countries in Africa, perceptions of probity levels in the country are worsening, following some recent high-profile arrests for alleged corruption.

In 2013, Mauritius placed 1st out of 52 African countries on the Mo Ibrahim Index of African Governance. With 82.9 points out of 100, Mauritius topped the list of Africa's best-governed nations for the seventh consecutive year. The average score for the African continent is 51.6 points.

In 2002, the government adopted the Prevention of Corruption Act, which led to the establishment of an Independent Commission Against Corruption (ICAC). ICAC has the power to investigate corruption and money laundering offenses and can also seize the proceeds of corruption and money laundering.

Anti-Corruption Resources

Some useful resources for individuals and companies regarding combating corruption in global markets include the following:

- Information about the U.S. Foreign Corrupt Practices Act (FCPA), including a "Lay-Person's Guide to the FCPA" is available at the U.S. Department of Justice's Website at: http://www.justice.gov/criminal/fraud/fcpa.

- Information about the OECD Antibribery Convention including links to national implementing legislation and country monitoring reports is available at: http://www.oecd.org/department/0,3355,en_2649_34859_1_1_1_1_1,00.html.

- See also new Antibribery Recommendation and Good Practice Guidance Annex for companies: http://www.oecd.org/dataoecd/11/40/44176910.pdf.

- General information about anticorruption initiatives, such as the OECD Convention and the FCPA, including translations of the statute into several languages, is available at the Department of Commerce Office of the Chief Counsel for International Commerce Website: http://www.commerce.gov/os/ogc/transparency-and-anti-bribery-initiatives.

- Transparency International (TI) publishes an annual Corruption Perceptions Index (CPI). The CPI measures the perceived level of public-sector corruption in 180 countries and territories around the world. The CPI is available at: http://www.transparency.org/policy_research/surveys_indices/cpi/2009. TI also publishes an annual *Global Corruption Report* which provides a systematic evaluation of the state of corruption around the world. It includes an in-depth analysis of a focal theme, a series of country reports that document major corruption related events and developments from all continents and an overview of the latest research findings on anti-corruption diagnostics and tools. See http://www.transparency.org/research/gcr.

- The World Bank Institute publishes Worldwide Governance Indicators (WGI). These indicators assess six dimensions of governance in 213 countries, including Voice and Accountability, Political Stability and Absence of Violence, Government Effectiveness, Regulatory Quality, Rule of Law and Control of Corruption. See http://info.worldbank.org/governance/wgi/index.asp. The World Bank Business Environment and Enterprise Performance Surveys may also be of interest and are available at: http://data.worldbank.org/data-catalog/BEEPS.

- The World Economic Forum publishes the *Global Enabling Trade Report*, which presents the rankings of the Enabling Trade Index, and includes an assessment of the transparency of border administration (focused on bribe payments and corruption) and a separate segment on corruption and the regulatory environment. See http://www.weforum.org/s?s=global+enabling+trade+report.

- Additional country information related to corruption can be found in the U.S. State Department's annual *Human Rights Report* available at http://www.state.gov/g/drl/rls/hrrpt/.

- Global Integrity, a nonprofit organization, publishes its annual *Global Integrity Report*, which provides indicators for 106 countries with respect to governance and anti-corruption. The report highlights the strengths and weaknesses of national level anti-corruption systems. The report is available at: http://report.globalintegrity.org/.

Bilateral Investment Agreements Return to top

In September 2006, Mauritius and the United States signed a Trade and Investment Framework Agreement (TIFA), aimed at strengthening and expanding trade and investment ties between the two countries. The TIFA Council, comprising of representatives from both governments, normally meets every year to identify impediments to trade and investments and propose new areas of collaboration.

Mauritius also has an investment incentive agreement with the Overseas Private Investment Corporation (OPIC).

Mauritius has signed Investment Promotion and Protection Agreements with the following 39 countries: Barbados, Belgium/Luxemburg Economic Union, Benin, Burundi, Cameroon, Chad, China, Comoros, Czech Republic, Finland, India, Indonesia, France, Germany, Ghana, Guinea, Madagascar, Mauritania, Mozambique, Nepal, Pakistan, Portugal, Republic of Korea, Romania, Rwanda, Senegal, Singapore, South Africa, Swaziland, Sweden, Switzerland, UK, Zimbabwe, Tanzania, Kenya, the Republic of Congo, Turkey, Kuwait and Gabon.

Bilateral Taxation Treaties

As of April 2014, Mauritius had signed Double Taxation Avoidance Treaties (DTATs) with the following countries: Belgium, Botswana, China, Croatia, Cyprus, France, Germany, India, Italy, Kuwait, Lesotho, Luxembourg, Madagascar, Malaysia, Mozambique, Namibia, Nepal, Oman, Pakistan, Russia, Rwanda, Senegal, Singapore, Sri Lanka, South Africa, Swaziland, Sweden, Thailand, United Kingdom, Zimbabwe, Uganda, Barbados, Seychelles, United Arab Emirates, Tunisia, Qatar, Bangladesh, Republic of Congo, Zambia, Kenya, Nigeria, Egypt, Monaco, Gabon, and Guernsey.

Mauritius has signed Tax Information Exchange Agreements (TIEAs) with Australia, Denmark, Finland, Norway, Guernsey, Faroe Islands, Greenland, Iceland and the United States.

In December 2013, Mauritius signed a Model 1A (reciprocal) Intergovernmental Agreement (IGA) to implement the provisions of the Foreign Account Tax Compliance Act (FATCA), the first such IGA signed in the African region.

OPIC and Other Investment Insurance Programs Return to top

Mauritius is eligible for the full range of OPIC investment insurance programs. It is also a member of the World Bank's Multilateral Investment Guarantee Agency.

Labor Return to top

In December 2013, Mauritius had a labor force estimated at 597,500, including 366,900 males and 230,600 females. Total employment stood at 552,000, including 26,300 foreign workers, mainly from China, India, Madagascar, Sri Lanka, Bangladesh, and South Africa. Most of them are employed in textile factories but some are in construction, tuna canning, and the hotel and catering sectors. The unemployment rate, which was 8.3 percent in 2011, fell to 8 percent in 2012, and remained at 8 percent in 2013, representing approximately 49,600 unemployed persons.

The GOM administratively establishes minimum wages, which vary according to the sector of employment, through the National Remuneration Board (NRB), and it mandates minimum wage increases annually based on inflation. Although trade unions often negotiate wages higher than those set by the NRB, the NRB issues Remuneration Orders for more than 90 percent of the workforce in the private sector.

In February 2009, the Employment Rights Act and the Employment Relations Act came into force. The main objectives were to revise and consolidate the existing labor and industrial relations laws, which were more than 30 years old, and to liberalize the labor market and enhance the effectiveness of collective bargaining. The new legislation also provided for the introduction of a Workfare Program under which laid-off workers benefit from government financial assistance for up to twelve months and will have opportunities for training to increase their employability.

Wages are low by Western standards but high by most Asian and African standards. The basic wages of factory workers in export-oriented enterprises range between USD 200 and USD 300 per month. Middle managers earn between USD 700 and USD 1,000 per month. Fringe benefits, including transport and meal allowances, paid leave, and bonuses, represent an additional 25 to 30 percent of basic wages.

While Mauritius has an active trade union movement, labor-management relations are generally good. Unionized workers, who account for less than 25 percent of the workforce, rarely disrupt business. There has not been a major strike since 1979, although under current legislation, unions have the legal right to do so. The government generally seeks to avoid strikes through a system that promotes settlement through negotiation or arbitration by the Employment Relations Tribunal and the National Remuneration Board. A National Tripartite Forum, comprised of representatives of government, employers and labor unions, has also been established to promote dialogue on issues of national interest, particularly those related to the workplace.

Workers' rights are protected under the Employment Rights Act 2008. Mauritius participates actively in the annual ILO conference in Geneva and adheres to ILO core conventions protecting workers' rights.

Foreign-Trade Zones/Free Ports Return to top

The Mauritius Freeport (free trade zone) established in 1992 is a customs-free zone for goods destined for re-export. The government's objective is to promote the country as a regional warehousing, distribution, marketing, and logistics center for eastern and southern Africa and the Indian Ocean rim. Through its membership in the Common Market for Eastern and Southern Africa (COMESA), the Southern African Development Community (SADC), and the Indian Ocean Commission (IOC), Mauritius offers preferential access to a market of over 400 million consumers, representing an import potential of USD 100 billion. Companies operating in the Freeport are exempt from corporate tax.

Situated on 52 hectares of land adjacent to the port facilities and a modern container terminal, the Freeport offers 120,000 square meters of infrastructure, including cold rooms, dry storage, an international trade exhibition center, processing units, and office space for transshipment, consolidation, storage, and processing activities. Freeport facilities are also available at the airport. Major shipping lines (i.e. Maersk/Sealand, P&O Nedloyd, and MSC) use Port Louis as a regional container transshipment hub, although improvements to the seaport are needed to increase shipping traffic.

Activities carried out in the Freeport include warehousing and storage, breaking bulk, sorting, grading, cleaning and mixing, labeling, packing and re-packing, minor processing, transshipment, cash and carry sales, export-oriented port based activities, export-oriented airport based activities, freight forwarding, express courier services, mail order, simple assembly, reshipment, and quality control and inspection services.

By the end of 2013, more than 260 Freeport companies were active in operations such as re-export, transshipment, minor processing, and assembly. In 2013, the Freeport imported USD 332 million and re-exported USD 311 million worth of goods. Main products re-exported include seafood (32 percent), machinery and transport equipment (23 percent), chemical and pharmaceutical products (15 percent), and beverages and tobacco (5.3 percent). In 2013, the principal export markets for the Freeport were Madagascar, Reunion Island, Hong Kong, United Arab Emirates, Japan, Spain, Singapore, Seychelles, and South Africa.

The Freeport sources its imports from a wide range of countries, including Hungary, China, India, Finland, Taiwan, France, Spain, and South Africa. The main products imported include fish, chemicals and pharmaceuticals, machinery, transport and telecommunication equipment, textile fabrics and accessories, ready-made garments, electrical goods, beverages and tobacco, and general consumer goods.

The Freeport facilities for warehousing, breaking bulk, and re-export should be of particular interest to American companies. These services enable businesses to ship containerized goods to Mauritius, warehouse them in secure, low-cost facilities, then break bulk and re-export them in an efficient and timely manner to African and Indian Ocean rim destinations. The private facility developers provide modern computerized warehousing, including cold rooms and processing centers. These include Freeport Operations (Mauritius) Ltd (www.freeport-operations.mu), Mauritius Freeport Development Co. Ltd (www.mfd.mu), and Froid Des Mascareignes (www.iblgroup.com/en/mascareignes).

Goods are assembled in the Freeport for export to the African and Indian Ocean markets. Current assembly and processing activities in the Freeport include jewelry and precious stones, PET plastic bottles, aluminum frames and fittings, transformation of fish into fillets, re-packaging of pharmaceuticals, and reconditioning of second-hand vehicles. The government is now seeking to promote more value-added activities in the Freeport.

The GOM, in collaboration with the private sector, has begun promoting the Freeport as a seafood hub, in particular focusing on the transshipment, processing, storage, distribution, and re-exportation of high value-added seafood products using the modern port and Freeport facilities and logistics. The government set up a "one-stop shop" in the port area to help facilitate administrative clearances related to the seafood industry. Thon des Mascareignes Ltd. (TDM), a leading Mauritian company in partnership with Spanish investors, is operating a tuna loin processing plant with a daily processing capacity of 250 tons for export to Europe and the U.S. for final processing and packaging. U.S. firm Bumble Bee Foods has a tuna supply and processing agreement with TDM.

The GOM wants to capitalize on the recent USD 360 million investment in the new airport terminal to promote the development of an "Aviation Hub," which will include cargo facilities. Airports of Mauritius Ltd, which is responsible for the development and administration of airport infrastructure, is currently expanding the Cargo and Freeport facilities at the airport over 72 hectares for a total amount of USD 17 million, scheduled for completion in July 2014.

Foreign Direct Investment Statistics Return to top

The following statistical tables, supplied by the Bank of Mauritius (Central Bank), show inflows of FDI in Mauritius by sector and country of origin (2010-2013).

Foreign Direct Investment by Sector 2010-2013 (USD million)

	2010	2011	2012	2013
Agriculture and Fishing	0	6.9	4.1	21.9
Manufacturing	2	1.8	14	9
Tourism	26.5	19.6	21	10.1
Financial	147	55.8	142	23.1
Real Estate	109	155	168	191
Health	87	0	0	0
Other	73.3	87.8	70.4	51.7
Total	444.8	326.9	419.5	306.8

Source: Bank of Mauritius (http://www.bom.mu)

Foreign Direct Investment by Country of Origin 2010-2013 (USD million)

	2010	2011	2012	2013
Dubai	10.7	12.5	10.9	7.3
France	50.7	111.5	83.4	87.4
Germany	0.1	0.34	0	7.7
Belgium	11	3.1	0.2	6.1
Luxembourg	8.1	1.7	0.1	6.3
Reunion	4.3	2.8	0.5	4.9
South Africa	46.6	73.5	91.7	48.3
Switzerland	18.7	1.7	4.9	18.2
U.K.	147	59.4	121	16.2
U.S.	4.2	7.8	12.7	6.8
South Asia	91.6	3.3	8.7	2.4
East Asia	20	6.9	64	61.5
Others	29.8	35.5	17.2	33.7
Total	442.8	320.04	415.3	306.8

Source: Bank of Mauritius

In 2013, total FDI inflows into Mauritius amounted to just less than USD 307 million, the main sources being France, China, and South Africa. Together these sources represented over 60 percent of total investments. The bulk of the FDI was directed to real estate, financial services, and fishing.

U.S. Investment in Mauritius

Mauriden Ltd., owned by a U.S. citizen, was one of the first companies to operate in the Export Processing Zone more than 35 years ago. Initially involved in diamond cutting and polishing, Mauriden now focuses on the production of jewelry for its duty free shops (Adamas).

Laurelton Diamonds (Mauritius) Ltd, a subsidiary of Tiffany & Co based in New York, started operations in 2008. Laurelton specializes in the cutting and polishing of diamonds that are exported to the United States for further transformation.

Apollo-Blake, with 100 percent U.S. ownership, started operations in 2008 as a Business Process Outsourcing (BPO) company that focuses on customer relations services, working primarily with U.S. and European clients.

Johnson & Johnson bought Perousse & Plastie Ltd, a French company based in Mauritius, in 2009. PP Sud Ltd, as the company is now called, specializes in the manufacture of silicone implants for cosmetic and reconstructive surgery.

MIC-USA Inc., a subsidiary of Millicom International Cellular, is a joint venture partner (50 percent shareholding) with local company, Emtel Ltd, in the provision of cellular phone service in Mauritius.

Ceridian (Mauritius) Ltd., a subsidiary of Ceridian Inc., specializes in software development and payroll and human resource solutions for European, U.S., and Canadian markets.

Microsoft and IBM have regional distribution offices in Mauritius, serving the Indian Ocean region, while HP Mauritius was officially launched in October 2011.

Also in 2011, Harley-Davidson opened an outlet and showroom in the north of the main island.

KFC, Pizza Hut, and McDonald's have been operating in Mauritius for a number of years, all through local franchisees.

Starwood Group currently manages three hotels in Mauritius, namely Le Meridien, St. Regis Mauritius Resort, and Westin Turtle Bay. Outrigger Mauritius Resort, owned by Outrigger Enterprises Group based in Hawaii, opened in January 2014.

Following more than two years of bidding and negotiations, California-based Synnove Energy opened an office in Mauritius in 2013 (or 2014??) to implement the construction and operations of a 4 megawatt solar power project.

Covance Laboratories Ltd, a subsidiary of Covance Inc., holds 47 percent of the share capital of Noveprim Ltd., a local company involved in the breeding of primates for export to U.S. and European medical research laboratories.

UPS and FedEx have offices in Mauritius.

Foreign Investment in Mauritius

In 2013 Sapmer, based in nearby Reunion Island (an overseas department of France), invested about USD 100 million in a new tuna processing plant that will process up to 21,000 tons of raw tuna annually. Sapmer already had a 50 percent stake in another fish processing plant/cold storage in joint venture with a local business group, IBL Ltd. Sapmer ordered five purse seiners (fishing vessels) for tuna fishing, estimated at USD 170 million. The construction of two of the five boats has been completed and one is already sailing under the Mauritian flag.

French company South Kasios relocated part of its production of bone substitutes from France to Mauritius in 2013. The bone substitutes are used in orthopedics, dental surgery and also during surgical interventions on the spine.

South African companies are investing heavily in various sectors of the Mauritian economy. Over the past six years South African FDI into Mauritius has grown significantly to reach a total of nearly USD 150 million by 2013. South African companies, in joint venture with Mauritian firms, have invested in property development (shopping malls, luxury apartments), retail trade (supermarkets, restaurants), and IT-enabled services.

A number of Indian and British universities have opened branches in Mauritius in the past couple of years, enrolling students from all over the region.

Several French, British, and Indian companies in joint ventures with Mauritian partners have invested in the ICT sector in Mauritius as a result of the government's determination to develop Mauritius into a regional ICT hub. Leading global players, including Accenture, Orange Business Services (France), InfoSys (India), Hinduja (India), Huawei (China), and TNT (U.K.) have operations in business process outsourcing activities, call centers, disaster recovery and business continuity centers, and software development.

Indian companies have made significant investment in the past several years. Indian Oil Ltd. built a 24,000 metric ton-fuel storage terminal as well as a testing laboratory. It also operates a number of retail distribution outlets in Mauritius.

Mahanagar Telephone Mauritius Ltd., an Indian telecom company, has been providing international long distance telephone service as well as fixed, mobile phone and wireless internet services for a number of years. Another Indian company, Bharat Telecom Ltd, holder of an Internet Service Provider (ISP) license, started its operations in October 2012.

Indian companies have also made substantial investment in the health sector. In 2007, Apollo Hospitals Group from India embarked on the construction of a high-tech 200-bed hospital in Mauritius, estimated at USD 30 million, in a joint venture with a local corporate group. The hospital began operations in July 2009. In December 2008, another Indian healthcare provider, Fortis Healthcare Ltd., invested approximately USD 2 million in the share capital of a well-known private local health clinic. Over the past two years, Fortis has opened a second clinic and has added new services, including neonatal and dental care. In 2010 Dr Agarwal's Eye Hospital from India set up a super-specialty eye hospital while the Challenge Hair Group opened a state-of-the-art medical center in Trou-aux-Biches for hair grafting, plastic and cosmetic surgery, and dentistry. Also in 2010, Parenteral Drugs (India) Ltd acquired a majority stake in a local pharmaceutical manufacturing company.

Various Indian hotel groups, including Oberoi, Sagar, and Taj have also invested in high-end hotels and resorts in Mauritius. In March 2010, Indian firm Patel Engineering was awarded the contract for the development of a new township (Neotown) at Les Salines, near Port Louis. However, the project, which was officially launched in March 2010, has yet to start.

The Jin Fei Economic and Trade Cooperation Zone, just north of the capital in Riche Terre, is one of five special economic zones in Africa announced by China in 2006. The aim was to encourage the Chinese business community to invest in Mauritius in order to access COMESA and SADC markets and trade preferences. Although the government of Mauritius has undertaken some basic infrastructural works, the project has yet to take off despite two re-brandings since 2006 and several grants and concessionary loans from the Chinese.

Outward Investment

In Mauritius, there are no restrictions on capital outflows. The bulk of direct outward investment over the past several years has gone to the tourism sector (hotel construction) in Maldives and Seychelles, the manufacturing sector (mainly apparel) in Madagascar, India and Bangladesh, and the banking sector in Seychelles, Madagascar, Reunion, Maldives, Mozambique, South Africa, and India. There are increasing investments by Mauritain sugar conglomerates into the agri-business sector in several African countries as well.

The Government of Mauritius supports regional integration. Following an offer from the Government of Mozambique of some 23,500 hectares of land, the government of Mauritius set up the Regional Development Co. Ltd (RDC). Its main objective is the promotion of regional food security and the implementation of other regional development projects. RDC has also incorporated a subsidiary in Mozambique, RDC Mozambique, which acts as the interface between potential investors and the government of Mozambique. Since 2011, RDC has issued at least two requests for proposals from potential investors for agricultural activities, including rice production and processing as well as renewable energy projects. Ghana also offered 30,000 hectares of land to Mauritius for the development of various agricultural and industrial activities. A local company is currently discussing sugar production, energy, and other agricultural activities with the authorities in Ghana.

The Mauritius Commercial Bank Ltd, the largest banking corporation in Mauritius, has established a strong presence in the Indian Ocean region with operations in Reunion, Madagascar, Seychelles, Mozambique, and the Maldives. They also have operations in France and a representative office in South Africa. The State Bank of Mauritius, another large local bank, has established banking operations in India and Madagascar, while AfrAsia Bank, established in 2007, purchased 35 percent of shares in a financial group in Zimbabwe in 2012.

Outward FDI in the garment industry emerged in 1990, when the low-end operations were relocated to lower-wage countries in the region. The African Growth and Opportunity Act (AGOA) also provided the impetus for several local textile companies to open factories in the region, mainly Madagascar and Mozambique. Ciel Textile Ltd, a leading Mauritian textile group, has garment-manufacturing operations in India and Bangladesh.

Other Mauritian investments on the African mainland relate to the use of expertise in the sugar industry to rehabilitate and manage sugar production in Mozambique, Tanzania, Ivory Coast, Madagascar, and Uganda. Long-established conglomerates like the Rogers Group, IBL Group, the Currimjee Group, the Food and Allied Industries Group, the Altima Group, and British-American Investment Ltd. have established businesses in the region in commerce, poultry, financial non-banking services and healthcare, principally in Madagascar, Mozambique, Kenya, and Uganda. Mauritius Telecom and Emtel, a subsidiary of the Currimjee group, have also invested in the telecommunications sector in Madagascar and Seychelles. In October 2011, Mauritius Telecom purchased 50 percent of the shareholding of Telecom Vanuatu Ltd, the telecom operator in the small Pacific island nation of Vanuatu. The State Informatics Limited operates a subsidiary company in Namibia and Botswana. In January 2014, Omnicane Ltd, a major local sugarcane conglomerate, signed a joint venture agreement with Hydroneo Afrique Ltd, a subsidiary of French group Mecamidi, for the development and construction of a number of hydro-electric power plants in East Africa over the next three years.

The following tables provide statistics on FDI outflows by country and sector of investment during the period 2010-2013.

Mauritius Direct Investment Abroad by Sector 2010-2013 (USD million)

	2010	2011	2012	2013
Agriculture	0.34	18	2.6	0
Tourism	31.8	14	29.8	77.3
Manufacturing	1	26.6	11.2	4
Real Estate	3.9	5.5	8.3	27.8
Financial	33.7	13	26.3	17.2
Health	43.6	0	0	0
Other	3.2	5.7	9	7.1
Total	117.54	82.8	87.2	133.4

Source: Bank of Mauritius

Mauritius Direct Investment Abroad by Country 2010-2013 (USD million)

	2010	2011	2012	2013
France	0.3	1.5	2.5	6.8
Switzerland	25	2	0	3.4
Reunion Island	3.4	2.3	1.8	2.1
U.S.	1.8	0.8	0.2	2.7
Madagascar	2.2	6.4	4.9	14.6

Maldives	1.2	0	0	0
South Africa	10.3	1.7	2.5	1.2
Dubai	0	1.4	0	5.2
South Asia	32.6	21.4	6.1	0.1
East Asia	0	5.6	3.8	1
Seychelles	3.5	2.6	0.1	0.8
Mozambique	0.3	22.7	2.5	0.1
Others	46.9	15.8	62.8	95.4
Total	127.5	84.2	87.2	133.4

Source: Bank of Mauritius

Key Macroeconomic data, U.S. FDI in Mauritius

- Economic Data from World Bank (http://www.worldbank.org/en/country/mauritius)

Year: 2012
GDP (Millions U.S. Dollars): 10,490

- U.S. FDI in Mauritius from Bureau of Economic Analysis (http://www.bea.gov)

Year	Amount (Millions U.S. Dollars, stock position)
2012	7,062

- Mauritius FDI in the United States from Bureau of Economic Analysis

Year	Amount (Millions U.S. Dollars, stock position)
2012	3,431

Sources and Destination of FDI from IMF (http://cdis.imf.org)

Mauritius, 2012

From Top Five Sources/To Top Five Destinations (US Dollars, Millions)

Inward Direct Investment			Outward Direct Investment		
Total Inward	282,103	100%	Total Outward	292,125	100%
Singapore	30,228	11%	India	105,604	36%
Netherlands	25,828	9%	Netherlands	23,792	8%
United States	24,329	9%	China, P.R.: Mainland	21,789	7%
United Kingdom	20,607	7%	Singapore	11,912	4%
India	18,636	7%	United Arab Emirates	7,235	2%
"0" reflects amounts rounded to +/- USD 500,000.					

Sources of Portfolio Investment from IMF (http://cpis.imf.org)

Mauritius, 2012

Top Five Partners (Millions, US Dollars)								
Total			**Equity Securities**			**Total Debt Securities**		
World	101,325	100%	World	91,562	100%	World	9,763	100%
India	78,228	77%	India	72,831	80%	India	5,396	55%
China, P.R.: Mainland	5,300	5%	China, P.R.: Mainland	4,687	5%	South Africa	884	9%
China, P.R.: Hong Kong	2,693	3%	China, P.R.: Hong Kong	2,670	3%	United States	731	7%
South Africa	2,509	2%	South Africa	1,626	2%	China, P.R.: Mainland	613	6%
Singapore	1,946	2%	Singapore	1,503	2%	Singapore	443	5%

Contact Point at Post   Return to top

NAME: Patrick Koucheravy
TITLE: Economic Officer
ADDRESS: Rogers House (4th floor), John Kennedy Avenue, Port Louis, Mauritius
TELEPHONE NUMBER: +230 202 4410
EMAIL ADDRESS: KoucheravyPE@state.gov

Return to table of contents

Chapter 7: Trade and Project Financing

- How Do I Get Paid (Methods of Payment)
- How Does the Banking System Operate
- Foreign-Exchange Controls
- U.S. Banks and Local Correspondent Banks
- Project Financing
- Web Resources

How Do I Get Paid (Methods of Payment)   Return to top

Mauritius has a well-developed financial system. Payments for import transactions are generally made through letters of credit, depending on the exporter's payment experience with the buyer. The terms of payment as well as the currency of payment should be clearly specified in these documents. An open account can be a convenient method of payment if the buyer is well established and has a favorable payment record. For new customers, it is advisable to do a credit check through the U.S. Department of Commerce International Company Profile. Interested U.S. firms should contact their nearest Export Assistance Center for additional information. More information can be found at http://export.gov/eac/index.asp.

How Does the Banking System Operate   Return to top

Mauritius has a relatively sophisticated banking sector with 23 banks currently licensed to undertake banking business. The Banking Act of 2004 provides for banking business to be conducted under a single banking license regime. Accordingly, all banks are free to conduct business in all currencies, including the Mauritian rupee. There are also several non-bank financial institutions, which are authorized to conduct deposit-taking business. The banking system is highly concentrated with two long-established domestic banking companies, Mauritius Commercial Bank (MCB) and State Bank of Mauritius (SBM) holding between them 65 percent of all banking assets. Foreign banks present in Mauritius include the Hong Kong and Shanghai Banking Corporation (HSBC), Barclays Bank, Bank of Baroda, Habib Bank, Banque des Mascareignes, PT Bank International Indonesia, Deutsche Bank, Standard Bank, Standard Chartered Bank, and Investec Bank.

The banks focus mostly on trade financing and on provision of working capital. Accounts may be opened in all major currencies as well as the Mauritian rupee. Several commercial banks offer card-payment services, such as credit and debit cards and direct debits. Other facilities, including phone banking, home banking, internet banking, and PC banking, are also provided by some banks. Commercial banks offer spot and forward transactions in all major currencies.

Commercial banks have diversified into non-banking business through subsidiaries and affiliates. Banks are engaged in the provision of leasing, stock brokering, asset and fund management, investment and private banking business, insurance agency, and portfolio and custodial management.

The Bank of Mauritius, which is the central bank, carries out the supervision and regulation of banks as well as non-bank financial institutions authorized to accept deposits. An updated Bank of Mauritius Act, which strengthened the central bank's institutional framework as well as its supervisory powers, was enacted in October 2004. It also has the power to establish prudential safety and soundness standards and regulations, and does so primarily by issue of Guidelines/Guidance Notes. The central bank has endorsed the Core Principles for Effective Banking Supervision as set out by the Basel Committee on Banking Supervision.

A list of banks operating in Mauritius, including their profiles as well as the Code of Banking Practice, is available at the website of the Mauritius Bankers Association: http://www.mba.mu/.

Foreign-Exchange Controls   Return to top

There are no foreign exchange controls in Mauritius.

U.S. Banks and Local Correspondent Banks   Return to top

There are no U.S. banks in Mauritius, although several of the leading banks have a large network of correspondent banks based in the major cities around the world, including New York.

Project Financing   Return to top

Most major infrastructure projects are financed by institutions such as the World Bank, the African Development Bank, the European Investment Bank, the French Agence Française de Développement, the Kuwait Fund, and the Arab Bank for Economic Development in Africa. Some are funded through bilateral assistance from France, India, China, Germany, and Japan. These sources fund a broad portfolio of projects, including port and airport upgrades, sewage treatment, road, bridge and dam construction, energy, telecommunications, hospital and housing construction, and sports facilities. Mauritius is eligible for the programs of both the Overseas Private Investment Corporation (OPIC) and the Export-Import Bank of the United States (Ex-Im). The U.S. Trade and Development Agency also provides grant funding for feasibility studies spanning a wide variety of sectors.

Web Resources   Return to top

Export-Import Bank of the United States: http://www.exim.gov

Country Limitation Schedule: http://www.exim.gov/tools/country/country_limits.html

OPIC: http://www.opic.gov

Trade and Development Agency: http://www.tda.gov/

SBA's Office of International Trade: http://www.sba.gov/oit/

USDA Commodity Credit Corporation: http://www.fsa.usda.gov/ccc/default.htm

U.S. Agency for International Development: http://www.usaid.gov

Mauritius Bankers Association: http://www.mba.mu

African Development Bank: http://www.afdb.org

Agence Française de Développent: http://www.afd.fr/home/pays/afrique/geo-afr/maurice

World Bank: http://www.worldbank.org or contact the World Bank"s local office:

World Bank, Medine Mews
Chaussee
Port Louis, Mauritius
Contact: Mr. Rafael Munoz Moreno, Country Representative
Tel: +230 208-0342
E-mail: wrabot@worldbank.org

Return to table of contents

Chapter 8: Business Travel

- Business Customs
- Travel Advisory
- Visa Requirements
- Telecommunications
- Transportation
- Language
- Health
- Local Time, Business Hours and Holidays
- Temporary Entry of Materials and Personal Belongings
- Web Resources

Business Customs   Return to top

Business customs are similar to those in Europe and the United States. For men, normal business wear is suit and tie. During the cooler months -- June through September -- light woolens are recommended. Humidity can be quite high during summer – November through April-- especially in the capital city and the coastal areas. Lunches and cocktail receptions are common business functions. Prospective visitors should bring an adequate supply of business cards as well as brochures and other literature.

Travel Advisory   Return to top

Mauritius' overall crime rate is medium and violent crimes involving tourists are relatively uncommon. Most criminal activity directed against foreigners is limited to non-violent petty crimes, such as "snatch thefts" in crowded shopping areas. Visitors are advised to keep a low profile and to not carry large sums of cash or wear expensive jewelry. If possible, leave wallets or purses secured at the hotel and carry only necessary cash and ID in a front pocket. Purses or shoulder bags should be closed and tucked under the arm and the strap held. Travelers are advised to refrain from walking alone at night outside hotel grounds.

For the latest Consular Information Sheet and travel advisory on Mauritius, please click on the following link: http://travel.state.gov/travel/cis_pa_tw/pa/pa_4787.html
For general information on international travel, please visit the main website at: http://www.travel.state.gov.

Visa Requirements   Return to top

Visas are not required for U.S. citizens, but travelers must have an onward or return ticket. Immunization certificates are not required unless the traveler arrives from an infected area.

Mauritian businesspeople traveling to the U.S. require visas. Visa applicants should go to the following links.

State Department Visa Website: http://travel.state.gov/visa/

U.S. Embassy Port Louis Consular Section: http://mauritius.usembassy.gov/consular_section.html.

Telecommunications Return to top

Mauritius has a telecommunications infrastructure that has not kept pace with recent technological advances. Reliable international mail, telephone, fax, e-mail, and internet services are available. Speed and bandwidth of internet connectivity, though improving, are inadequate for many modern commercial requirements. Main players in the telecommunications services market include Mauritius Telecom, (a government entity that operates in partnership with France Telecom), Emtel Ltd, and Mahanagar Telephone (Mauritius) Ltd, an Indian company. In addition, quick overseas deliveries can be effected through the Mauritius Postal Service or services such as FedEx, UPS, DHL, and TNT.

Transportation Return to top

Mauritius is connected to several cities around the world through direct air flights. Regular flights serve Europe, Southern Africa, India, East Asia, Australia, and the United Arab Emirates. There are no direct flights between Mauritius and the United States. U.S. travelers typically transit Paris, London, Johannesburg or Dubai. It is also relatively easy to travel within the island by taxi or rental car. In general taxis are equipped with meters, but fares may be negotiated before setting out. Traffic drives on the left. Port Louis is a 50-minute drive from the airport and easily accessible from other parts of the island except during the morning and evening rush hours.

Language Return to top

The official language is English, but French and Creole are used in everyday life. Most business executives are bilingual in English and French. A number of Asian languages (Hindi, Urdu, and Mandarin) are also spoken.

Health Return to top

Mauritius has no major health hazards. It is considered malaria-free. Hospitals and clinics within the public medical system are adequate and free. Apollo Bramwell Hospital, a private hospital (of Apollo Group of Hospitals, India), was opened in 2009. In 2008, another Indian healthcare provider, Fortis Healthcare Ltd., invested in another well-known local clinic now called Fortis-Darne Clinic. In addition, there are a number of other private clinics that offer adequate medical care.

Local Time, Business Hours, and Holidays Return to top

Local Time and Business Hours: Local time is four hours ahead of Greenwich Mean Time and eight hours ahead of Eastern Standard Time. Business hours are as follows: Government Offices: 0900-16.00 Monday thru Friday

Banks: 09.00-15.00 Monday thru Friday (some banks remain open until 5.00 p.m. on Fridays)

Businesses: 09.00-16.30 Monday thru Friday; 09.00-13.00 Saturday

There are 15 Mauritian public holidays. The following are fixed: New Years, January 1 and 2; Independence Day, March 12; Labor Day, May 1; Assumption, August 15; Arrival of Indentured Labor, November 2, and Christmas, December 25. The remaining holidays are religious festivals whose dates vary. The American Embassy is closed on American and local holidays.

Temporary Entry of Materials and Personal Belongings Return to top

No duty is levied on necessary and appropriate apparel and personal effects of a passenger arriving in Mauritius. Articles that are in excess of the concessions and allowances listed below are liable for duty.

A passenger 18 years of age or over may bring the following goods, free of customs duty: tobacco (including cigars and cigarettes) not exceeding 250 grams, spirits not exceeding 1 liter, wine, ale, or beer not exceeding 2 liters total.

In addition to allowances and concessions above, a tourist may bring with him/her the following goods free of customs duty:

- One portable musical instrument
- One portable sound and/or image recorder
- One portable radio receiver
- One portable video camera
- One camera
- One sporting firearm with not more than 50 cartridges (police permit is required before importation)
- One non-powered bicycle
- One windsurfer and up to three assorted sails
- One surf board
- Fishing equipment, excluding any type of underwater fishing gun

Information on customs formalities is available at
http://mra.gov.mu/index.php/faq/custom#2

Web Resources Return to top

State Department Visa Website: http://travel.state.gov/visa/index.html

U.S. Embassy Consular Section: http://mauritius.usembassy.gov/consular_section.html

Mauritius Revenue Authority: http://mra.gov.mu/index.php/faq/custom#2

The Embassy's Economic/Commercial Section in Port Louis, Mauritius can be contacted via email at: jathoonisx@state.gov or caunhyerx@state.gov; Phone: +230 202-4464 or +230 202-4430; Fax: +230 208-9534 or visit our website http://mauritius.usembassy.gov.

Return to table of contents

Return to table of contents

Chapter 9: Contacts, Market Research and Trade Events

- Contacts
- Market Research
- Trade Events

Contacts Return to top

U.S. Embassy, Port Louis, Mauritius: http://mauritius.usembassy.gov

U.S. Commercial Service, South Africa: http://export.gov/southafrica/

Government of Mauritius Portal: http://www.gov.mu

Government of Mauritius Ministries and Departments:
http://www.gov.mu/English/GovernmentBodies/Pages/default.aspx

Board of Investment: http://www.investmauritius.com

Mauritius Chamber of Commerce and Industry: http://www.mcci.org

The Embassy's Economic/Commercial Section in Port Louis, Mauritius can be contacted via email at: jathoonisx@state.gov or caunhyerx@state.gov; Phone: +230 202 4464 or +230 202 4430; Fax: +230 208 9534 or visit our website http://mauritius.usembassy.gov.

Market Research Return to top

To view market research reports produced by the U.S. Commercial Service please go to the following website: http://www.export.gov/mrktresearch/index.asp and click on Country and Industry Market Reports.

Please note that these reports are only available to U.S. citizens and U.S. companies. Registration to the site is required, and is free.

Trade Events

Return to top

Please click on the link below for information on upcoming trade events.

http://www.export.gov/tradeevents/index.asp

Return to table of contents

Chapter 10: Guide to Our Services

The President's National Export Initiative marshals Federal agencies to **prepare U.S. companies to export successfully**, **connect them with trade opportunities** and **support them once they do have exporting opportunities**.

The U.S. Commercial Service offers customized solutions to help U.S. exporters, particularly small and medium sized businesses, successfully expand exports to new markets. Our global network of trade specialists will work one-on-one with you through every step of the exporting process, helping you to:

- Target the best markets with our world-class research
- Promote your products and services to qualified buyers
- Meet the best distributors and agents for your products and services
- Overcome potential challenges or trade barriers
- Gain access to the full range of U.S. government trade promotion agencies and their services, including export training and potential trade financing sources

To learn more about the Federal Government's trade promotion resources for new and experienced exporters, please click on the following link: www.export.gov.

For more information on the services the U.S. Commercial Service offers to U.S. exporters, please click on the following link:
http://export.gov/southafrica/servicesforu.s.companies/index.asp.

The U.S. Embassy to Mauritius and Seychelles in Port Louis, Mauritius is a U.S. Commercial Service Partner Post. The Economic/Commercial team in Port Louis works closely with the U.S. Commercial Service based in Johannesburg, South Africa and can provide detailed information on the local market. For more information, please contact us via email at: jathoonisx@state.gov or caunhyerx@state.gov; Phone: +230 202-4464 or +230 202-4430; Fax: +230 208-9534 or visit our website
http://mauritius.usembassy.gov/business.html.

U.S. exporters seeking general export information/assistance or country-specific commercial information can also contact the **U.S. Department of Commerce's Trade Information Center** at **(800) USA-TRAD(E)**.